Kathryn Kuhlman

Her Spiritual Legacy and
Its Impact on My Life

Benny Hinn

THOMAS NELSON PUBLISHERS
NASHVILLE

Published in Nashville, Tennessee, by Thomas Nelson, Inc.

Scripture quotations are from the
NEW KING JAMES VERSION of the Bible.
Copyright © 1979, 1980, 1982,
Thomas Nelson, Inc., Publishers
and from the
The Holy Bible, KING JAMES VERSION.

ISBN: 0-7852-7888-5

Printed in the United States of America.
1 2 3 4 5 6 7 - 03 02 01 00 99 98

This book is dedicated to those whose
lives were touched by the Holy Spirit through the
ministry of Kathryn Kuhlman — and to their
children and their children's children.

Contents

Special Foreword by
Oral Roberts

I first heard of Kathryn Kuhlman in the 1960s while we were in California producing a television special at the NBC Burbank studios. Our director, Dick Ross told me about her and the following Sunday I attended one of Miss Kuhlman's services in Los Angeles.

In that meeting God's Spirit came over me as I saw the Lord working tremendous miracles of healing through her. I wept for joy and knew God had raised up this precious handmaiden of the Lord — one unequaled in my generation.

She brought forth the Word of Knowledge greater than I had seen. Immediately, I saw this gift of the Spirit in a new light and knew in my heart God was going to release it to His people everywhere. I believe it was a signal God was sending: "I Am that I Am — here as in the days of old. Listen to Me. Let you faith go to Me and see the wonders of My grace." And I believe it even more today. I feel that God, through Kathryn Kuhlman, brought the gift of the Word of Knowledge to prominence and it is being manifested more and more.

Kathryn's ministry at Oral Roberts University stirred our faculty and students to tears and to an understanding that God was visiting us. We have not been the same since. We have a profound sense of gratitude to God and to her.

Evelyn and I were blessed by being able to know Kathryn Kuhlman personally and considered her a dear, dear friend. She was certainly a peer in the miracle ministry and we loved her.

As the final hours of her life drew near at the Hillcrest Hospital in Tulsa, she asked us not to pray for her to be raised up, but rather that she would be released to go to her Heavenly Father. I was deeply moved, and not offended, as she would point a finger upward, signaling, "I want to go home." We honored her desire.

When my surgeon friend Dr. Bill Loughridge came from the operating room, he told me, "We had a perfect surgery but she really wants to go home. It's up to her now." I could feel the strong presence of God in that hospital, yet also a personal sadness since we wanted her to stay.

Kathryn's ministry affected me personally and positively since she lived in the presence of God — something I had experienced myself. It was as if two servants of God knew each other in a higher bond of God's miraculous power.

She also touched our son Richard, greatly encouraging him

as he was entering the healing ministry. The manifestation of the Word of Knowledge through him today could be traced back to her influence on his life. For that we thank God.

In the Kathryn Kuhlman services I was privileged to attend, I witnessed the miracle-working power of God. I saw people who were totally crippled stand to their feet and literally run through the audience.

As the years have passed, I continue to revere her life, her ministry, and her legacy. Among those of us especially called into the miracle/healing ministry, no one holds a higher place in my heart. Her prayer still rings in my ears and in my spirit. "Holy Spirit, let me never disobey my Lord."

There was none like her, yet I see the power of God that was on Miss Kuhlman descending on others today. Her very special son in the Lord, Benny Hinn, who was captured by the same Holy Spirit she knew, is carrying on her legacy. To see my dear friend Benny is to see Kathryn again in many ways. He has been anointed to move great masses into the power of the Holy Spirit unprecedented in our time. I feel doubly honored to have known and love both of them. I consider Benny Hinn "Number One" on the field of evangelism today. And, thank God, his work has just begun.

—Oral Roberts

Special Foreword by
Rex Humbard

Christmas, 1953, was a very difficult time for myself, my wife, Maude Aimee, and our two small children. We were struggling to begin construction of the Cathedral of Tomorrow in Akron, Ohio, and times were tough. One morning, just before Christmas Day, we looked out our front window in time to see a long black car pull into our drive. When the door opened, a tall, beautiful and gracious lady stepped out carrying an armful of gifts for our children and the family. This wonderful person was none other than Kathryn Kuhlman. We had known her less than a year, yet from those days until the time of her home-going, Kathryn was one of our dearest friends and shared with us in our triumphs and sorrows as we ministered the Gospel of Jesus Christ.

A few months earlier, in the summer of 1952, the Humbard family was conducting a city-wide crusade in our 6,000-seat Gospel Tent in Akron, Ohio. Following our first Saturday night service, two ladies asked to see me. I recognized one of them as a longtime friend, Myrtle Parrott, whom we first met in Dallas, Texas, in 1939. She introduced me to her sister, Kathryn Kuhlman, and said, "I am sure you have heard of her ministry." To the contrary, I had not heard of Miss Kuhlman. As we talked, Kathryn mentioned that she would like to use our tent for services on Sunday mornings. I told her I had never been in one of her meetings and would like very much to come to Youngstown where she was ministering and be a part of one of her services.

I arrived at the Stambaugh Auditorium in Youngstown, Ohio, early on Sunday morning and the building was already crowded to overflowing. When Miss Kuhlman walked on the stage, the presence of the Holy Spirit descended upon that place like a heavy fog. And for more than three hours she ministered, preached, sang, conducted a healing service and finally — and most important to me — gave an altar call for those who needed to know Jesus as their personal Savior.

As she gave this simple call for salvation, the entire front of the auditorium was filled with those making a profession of faith. In that one service, over one thousand people gave their hearts to the Lord. I gladly told Miss Kuhlman that she could use our tent and I would do anything to help her in this work that God had called her to do. At that point, Kathryn announced, "I will be in Akron, Ohio, Sunday morning at

11:00 A.M. in the Humbard Revival Tent."

Little did we know what was in store for us that next Sunday. At 4:30 A.M. the police came to our home and advised us that the tent was full and I needed to get there immediately to help with the crowd control. At 7:30 in the morning, Kathryn Kuhlman began her service which lasted for more than six hours. Lives were changed, bodies were healed, souls were saved and from that time forward, the work which was started in Akron would never be the same.

The next morning, the Akron *Beacon Journal* reported that over 18,000 people were in attendance. Every seat was taken, thousands stood inside the tent, and lines of people surrounded the entire area trying in every way they could to be a part of this mighty work of the Lord. This was the greatest move of God's Spirit I had ever seen! Kathryn came back to Akron many more Sundays and continued to minister the Gospel of Christ in her own special way.

Many years later, I had the privilege of ministering once again with Kathryn Kuhlman at the Anaheim Convention Center in southern California. Many thousands were in attendance and although she was in failing health and was soon to meet our Lord face to face, she conducted the service just as she had so many years ago in the Gospel Tent in Akron. Once again, the wonderful Spirit of the Lord fell upon the

Convention Center and lives were forever changed.

In my more than 66 years of full-time ministry, four great religious leaders have had a profound impact on my life.

- Dr. Billy Graham, who I have known for more than 50 years.
- Oral Roberts, who in 1949 prayed the prayer of faith for the healing of our oldest son, Rex, Jr., who suffered from tuberculosis and was healed.
- Kathryn Kuhlman, probably the closest friend my wife, Maude Aimee, and I have ever had, touched our lives in a wonderful and personal way.
- Benny Hinn, who I have had the privilege of ministering with in his crusade meetings throughout the United States and Canada.

Pastor Hinn received much of his inspiration and spiritual foundation from attending the meetings of Kathryn Kuhlman. As I sit on the platform of Benny Hinn's crusade meetings, I can sense the same spirit and feeling that I did many years ago during the services of Miss Kuhlman. Healings take place throughout the auditoriums and wonderful testimonies are told of those who have claimed their miracle while attending Pastor Hinn's meetings. Most important, I see the wonderful anointed altar calls for salvation just as I did in 1952 when I first attended the services of Kathryn at the Stambaugh Auditorium in Youngstown, Ohio.

The work that was begun those many years ago continues today through the ministry of Pastor Benny Hinn. Our prayer is that the days ahead will be the greatest that Benny Hinn has ever known because of his faithfulness to God's work and the principles that were learned at the feet of one of God's great servants, Kathryn Kuhlman.

— Rex Humbard

Chapter One

Dying a
Thousand Deaths

I tried to swallow, but my throat was parched. A vice-like knot gripped my stomach and my legs felt numb — almost paralyzed. Never in my twenty-four years had I been so frightened.

Finally I summoned the courage to pull back the heavy stage curtain of Pittsburgh's Carnegie Music Hall for a quick glance. The auditorium was filled with people who had come — some from great distances — to attend a memorial service in honor of Kathryn Kuhlman. It was 1977, one year after the famous woman evangelist had passed away.

These were her people, and they loved her dearly. After all, Pittsburgh had been the home of her ministry for nearly three decades. She had become an institution in the Steel City, lauded by city fathers and embraced by thousands from every level of society.

"Why me?" I wondered, still frozen in fright. Nobody knew who I was. Why had I been asked to minister at this unique and significant event? Three years earlier I had yet to preach my first sermon. I was a novice. And now this!

> THREE YEARS EARLIER I HAD YET TO PREACH MY FIRST SERMON. I WAS A NOVICE. AND NOW THIS!

Earlier that day I was asked to come to the Carlton House, which housed the offices of the Kathryn Kuhlman Foundation. After a few pleasantries, Maggie Hartner, who had been Kathryn's closest friend and associate, called me aside and gave me some well-seasoned advice. Quietly, she told me, "Now don't go and pray and get so tied up in yourself and your own needs that God can't use you tonight." And she added, "Go take a nap or something."

I could hardly believe what I was hearing. Asking me not to pray? I thought, "This has to be the most unusual advice I've ever been given!"

Leaving the building, I said to myself, "She doesn't know what she's talking about. Take a nap when I should be praying? No way! I'm going to pray whether she likes it or not!" And, not understanding Maggie's perspective, that's exactly what I did.

As soon as I returned to my hotel room, I began to pray diligently for the service that evening. Oh, how I prayed. For five hours I bombarded heaven in prayer. And then I was ready to go and do it for Jesus!

Pacing, Pacing

An hour before the service, Jimmie McDonald arrived at the hotel. This outstanding singer had been on the platform with Miss Kuhlman during the last fifteen years of her ministry. As we drove to Carnegie Auditorium together he outlined the program that was planned for the evening — what the choir would be singing and what he had prepared for his own music ministry.

A feature of the memorial event would be the showing of the Kathryn Kuhlman miracle service shot on location in Las Vegas in May, 1975. It was the only professionally directed film Miss Kuhlman ever allowed to be produced that featured one of her services.

We arrived at Carnegie Auditorium and Jimmie disappeared for a moment to take care of some last minute details. As I waited for him to return, I took a moment to savor my surroundings. Carnegie Auditorium was a beautiful building with gorgeous balconies and lovely decor. From behind the curtain I could hear the music of the Kathryn Kuhlman choir. It was so exciting to be there, and I felt especially honored to be part of it since hardly anyone knew who I was.

While the choir was rehearing, Jimmie returned to offer some final words of instruction. "Now Benny, after the film I'm going to lead the audience in one chorus of, *Jesus, Jesus, There's Just Something About That Name.* That will be your cue to walk on."

I nodded in agreement.

Jimmie vanished through the curtains and shortly thereafter the service began.

While the film was being shown I was pacing back and forth in that darkened backstage, almost overcome with anxiety. Suddenly, I remembered hearing Kathryn Kuhlman talk about her own battles before a miracle service.

My memory was jolted. I could almost hear her utter the words, "There are four steps that lead up to a little landing where the door opens on the stage of Carnegie Auditorium in Pittsburgh. There is a black doorknob on the door. I have walked up those four steps many times and have stood on that landing with my hand on that black doorknob and Kathryn Kuhlman has died a thousand deaths on that one spot."

Why would she make such an admission? In her words, "Because I knew that when I opened the door, sitting out there in that auditorium were people who had traveled hundreds of miles. People who had made sacrifices to be in that miracle service. There were people out there who'd come because it was their last resort. The medical profession could do nothing more for them. And they had come saying, 'We'll go into one of those miracle services and we'll believe God to answer prayer.'"

I could hear Miss Kuhlman continue, "I knew that sitting out there in that audience there would be a father who had taken off work. And he had come with his wife, with a little child. They'd tried everything. Perhaps it was cancer in that child's body. And that child was more precious to them than anything else in the world."

Then she said, "I knew standing on that top step I had no power to heal if my life depended on it. Oh, the helplessness of it all — the utter helplessness. And the complete dependence on the power of the Holy Spirit. I died not once, not twice, not a half dozen times. But over and over again."

Now it was my turn.

"Where Were You?"

As the film ended, Jimmie McDonald began leading the song that was planned. That meant it was almost time for me to walk on stage. Once more, I peeked at the crowd from my vantage point backstage and I was terrified. For the second time I heard the audience singing *Jesus, Jesus, There's Just Something About That Name.* Then the third. Finally Jimmie announced — more to me than to the audience — "We're going to sing this once more; then Benny Hinn is going to come out."

Since most of the people didn't know me, Jimmie gave a flattering, formal introduction concluding with, "Will you give a big Pittsburgh welcome to Benny Hinn!"

It took every muscle I could muster to walk on that stage. I walked slowly toward Jimmie. He whispered, "Where were you?" as he disappeared behind the curtains.

I was so nervous I couldn't speak, so I decided to lead the audience in the chorus once more. What I didn't realize, however, was that the musicians had changed the key and started playing another song. As I began to lead the audience in the familiar lyrics of *Jesus, Jesus, There's Just Something About That Name*, I became painfully aware that the key was too high. It was a disaster. Nobody could sing with me and I was struggling by myself, embarrassed beyond words.

Inside I was begging, "Please, let this service end. I've got to get out of here and go home."

After about thirty minutes that seemed like an eternity I finally threw my arms in the air and cried aloud, "I can't do it! Lord, I can't do it!"

At that precise moment I heard a voice deep inside me that said, "I'm glad you can't. Now I will."

Instantly, the apprehension and fear vanished. My physical body relaxed. I began to speak words I hadn't prepared and the power of God began to touch people across the auditorium. It was a memorable, moving evening.

> "IT'S NOT YOUR PRAYERS, IT'S NOT YOUR ABILITY, IT'S YOUR SURRENDER."

After the service Maggie shared something with me that I will always remember: "Kathryn always said, 'It's not your prayers, it's not your ability, it's your surrender.' Benny, just learn to surrender."

23

I was so exhausted and drained by the experience of that evening, I answered, "I don't think I know how."

Maggie Hartner replied, "Well, you had your first experience tonight."

For the next three years I held miracle services several times each year at the Carnegie Music Hall and the Soldiers and Sailors Memorial Hall, sponsored by the Kathryn Kuhlman Foundation.

The Shaking Wouldn't Stop

Over the years I have shared a portion of how God used Miss Kuhlman to dramatically influence and transform my life. Her impact, however, was far greater than most people can comprehend.

It was in that same city on Friday, December 21, 1973, that I arrived on a charter bus from Toronto to attend one of her miracle services at First Presbyterian Church.

As a 21-year-old who had become a born-again Christian nearly two years earlier, my journey had already taken some surprising turns. After being raised in a Greek Orthodox home in Jaffa, Israel, and being taught by nuns at a Catholic school, our family emigrated to Toronto when I was fifteen. Four years later, after being invited to attend a student-led prayer group at Georges Vanier public school, I asked Christ to become my personal Savior.

From that moment forward I was like a spiritual sponge — soaking in everything I could. The church I attended in downtown Toronto was home to nearly three thousand charismatic young people. In their exuberant worship they raised their hands, sang in the Spirit, and prayed in tongues. While I enjoyed their meetings of praise, and looked forward to each one with great anticipation, I was desperately seeking more of God. My heart seemed to be crying out, "Lord, is that all there is?"

> FROM THAT MOMENT FORWARD I WAS LIKE A SPIRITUAL SPONGE — SOAKING IN EVERYTHING I COULD.

One day God placed a Spirit-filled Free Methodist minister in my path. His name was Jim Poynter. "Benny," he asked, "have you ever heard of the ministry of Kathryn Kuhlman?"

"Oh, is that the woman who is on television and wears those long white dresses?" I responded. I remembered seeing her program once or twice, yet I wasn't especially attracted to her dramatic style.

"Well, I think you need to be in one of her services and see her ministry in person," said Poynter. He told me about the bus he had arranged and wanted me to join the group. I agreed to go.

Driving through a near-blizzard, we finally reached our hotel in Pittsburgh late in the evening. "Benny, I think we need to be at the church by six in the morning if we want a decent seat," said Jim. With only four hours of sleep and in the darkness of morning we arrived at the church. Several hundred people were already there, waiting for the doors to open two hours later. "Is it always like this?" I asked some people around us. "Every week," one woman replied.

The morning was bitter cold, but I was prepared — bundled up with layers of clothing plus gloves, boots, and a hat. Suddenly, however, my body began to vibrate as if someone was shaking me. "It can't be the weather," I thought, because I actually felt warm under my clothing. I pulled my coat close to me and waited in the cold morning. The longer I stood there the more the shaking continued uncontrollably. I could feel it in my legs, my arms, even my mouth. "What is happening to me?" I wondered.

"Benny, when those doors open, take off running as fast as you can to get a front seat," advised Jim. "If you don't move quickly they'll run right over you."

About a minute later, an usher opened the door and I sprinted to the front of the church like I was in a 100-yard dash — only to be told that the first row had already been reserved. The second row was filled, but Jim and I found an excellent spot on row three.

I removed my heavy clothing and tried to relax. I wasn't cold anymore, yet the shaking in my body would not go away. Frankly, I was beginning to worry. This unusual sensation seemed more than physical. Something was happening inside me and I was too embarrassed to tell Jim about it.

How Can I Explain It?

The music began and suddenly the lady evangelist with flaming red hair and a long white dress appeared on the platform. To say the atmosphere was *charged* does not begin to describe what I felt that morning. The entire audience began singing *How Great Thou Art* and, from the first note, tears began flowing down my cheeks. My hands were

> NEVER IN MY CHRISTIAN WALK HAD I EXPERIENCED ANYTHING LIKE THIS.

27

extended high into the air and I felt as if I was being bathed in glory. Never in my Christian walk had I experienced anything like this. Then, when the song ended, so did the shaking in my body.

I stood there quietly, continuing to worship the Lord. In that holy atmosphere, I felt a slow, gentle breeze begin to blow. I opened my eyes to look around for the source. I glanced up and there were no windows open. Yet I could feel this unusual wind moving down one arm and up the other, again and again, like a wave. It continued for several minutes and then I felt as if my entire body was wrapped in a warm, soothing blanket. It was incredible. I thought, "How can I ever explain this to anyone?"

> "DEAR JESUS, PLEASE HAVE MERCY ON ME." I SAID IT AGAIN AND AGAIN.

As Miss Kuhlman began to minister, I was lost in the Spirit, whispering, "Dear Jesus, please have mercy on me." I said it again and again, and as I whispered this prayer, it seemed as if a spotlight was shining down on my faults, my weaknesses and my sins. Then I heard the Lord's gentle voice say, "My mercy is abundant on you."

28

For the first time in my life, I was communing with God. He was talking with me, showing me His mercy and love. Absolutely nothing that had happened in my life could compare to that glorious moment.

The previous evening, on our journey to Pittsburgh, Jim told me about the miracles that took place in Miss Kuhlman's meetings. "She doesn't have a healing line," he explained. "And she doesn't lay hands on people personally. When the anointing of the Holy Spirit comes, people are wonderfully healed and they simply come forward to give their testimonies."

Jim had tried to prepare me, yet I had never witnessed such a display of God's miracle-working power. Deaf people could suddenly hear. A woman got out of her wheelchair and walked. There were scores of testimonies from people who were being healed of tumors, eye problems, arthritis, and other infirmities.

At one point in the service I looked up to see Miss Kuhlman with her face buried in her hands, sobbing. The music stopped. No one moved for what seemed like several minutes. Absolute silence. Then, in a flash, she threw back her head and thrust her long, bony finger forward with a boldness and authority that defy description. "P-l-e-a-s-e," she pleaded. "Please don't grieve the Holy Spirit." Still sobbing, she said, "Don't you understand? He's all I've got!" And she continued, "Please! Don't wound Him. He's all I've got. Don't wound the

One I love!"

She took a deep breath and extended her finger over the pulpit. It seemed she was pointing directly at me as she declared, "He's more real than anything in this world! He's more real to me than you are!"

In that moment, for the first time, I realized that the Holy Spirit was not an "it." He was a person, and, more than anything in the world, I longed to know Him.

All the way back to Toronto my mind replayed the scene of Miss Kuhlman leaning over the pulpit, saying, "He's more real to me than you are." It made me long to know Him too.

He's a Person!

That night, in my bedroom at our family home, I couldn't sleep. My mind was whirling with what I had experienced — the miracles and the words spoken by this unusual servant of God.

Suddenly I felt something pulling me out of my bed to the floor. I fell to my knees and the first words that came out of my mouth were, "Holy Spirit."

Speaking to Him as a person was totally new to me. I had talked to God, and to His Son, but until now I had never realized that the Holy Spirit was a living, real person.

Not knowing what would happen, I began to speak out

loud. "Holy Spirit," I began, "Kathryn says You are her Friend. I don't think I know You. Before today, I thought I did. But after that meeting I realize I really don't. Can I meet You? Can I really meet You?"

I had no idea what to expect. Would He answer? If so, how?

At first there was complete silence. Nothing happened. Then, a few minutes later, as I sat on the floor of my room with my eyes closed, suddenly I began to shake and vibrate all over — just as it happened outside the church in Pittsburgh, as I waited for the service to begin. I was tingling with the power of God's Spirit. He was there, present in my room. I could feel Him.

> HE WAS THERE, PRESENT IN MY ROOM. I COULD FEEL HIM.

After the most peaceful night's rest I could remember, I woke up and did what seemed to be the most natural thing in the world. I said, "Good morning, Holy Spirit."

From that dawn to this day He has been my Teacher, my Counselor, my Comforter, and my closest Friend.

"Have You Been Waiting for Me?"

My life began to change dramatically. Day after day, night

31

after night I became absorbed in God's Word. I would open my Bible and the Holy Spirit would literally cause my eyes to fall on a certain passage of Scripture, then another. He enlarged my understanding and caused the Word to come alive.

> THERE WAS A
> LITTLE RADIO
> NEXT TO MY BED,
> AND EVERY
> NIGHT I TUNED
> IT TO WWVA.

There was a little radio next to my bed and every night I tuned it to WWVA, a 50,000 watt station from Wheeling, West Virginia. Its powerful signal not only reached into Canada, but up and down the eastern United States, and as far away as Europe.

I knew I had the right frequency when I heard Kathryn Kuhlman's voice with her familiar sign-on: "Hello there! And have you been waiting for me?" Actually, in her style of over-pronouncing words, it was more like, "Helloooooooo theeeere! And have you been waaaaaiting for me?" Then she would usually add, "It so nice of you. I just knew you would be there."

Night after night she fed my soul, returning again and again to the theme that seemed to anchor her ministry. She called it "the greatest Power in the world" — the Holy Spirit.

Miss Kuhlman often laughed about her style as being "Missouri corn bread" because it was so down-to-earth. It may have been plain, yet her words were profound, and they touched something deep within me.

I can still hear her voice coming into my room, saying, "You may ask, 'How can I be filled with the Spirit?' I will give you the answer in just a few words: 'Turn yourself and all you have over to Jesus.' You may wonder, 'Is it just that simple?' It's just that simple."

Without question, the two greatest factors in my early spiritual growth were the Holy Spirit and Kathryn Kuhlman — in that order.

I took every opportunity to return to her Friday morning meetings. If a charter bus from Canada was going to one of her miracle services in Ottawa, Cleveland, or Buffalo, I did my best to be on board.

Not long after my encounter with the Holy Spirit, I was back at First Presbyterian in Pittsburgh and listened intently as Kathryn told of the price she had paid for the power of the Holy Spirit. Her message centered on the necessity of death to self. I can still see her looking across that audience, saying, "Any of you ministers can have what I have if you'll only pay the price."

She quoted from Isaiah 52 when God said, "Awake, awake! Put on your strength, O Zion." She explained that the words "Awake, awake!" mean "Pray, pray." Just as the Lord told us to "watch and pray" (Matthew 26:41). Through the years, this message has taken on a greater meaning for me. The personal cost Miss Kuhlman talked about was prayer — and I made a decision in that meeting that I would pay the price. It was the key to unleashing God's power.

> THE LORD ALLOWED EVERY MESSAGE, EVERY MIRACLE SERVICE AND EVERY RADIO PROGRAM TO BECOME SEEDS. THEY WERE SOWN INTO MY LIFE.

The Lord allowed every message, every miracle service and every radio program to become seeds. They were sown into my life. They grew. They blossomed. He used Kathryn to prepare me for ministry.

"I'll Be There!"

In late November 1975, I received a phone call from Maudie Phillips, the Canadian representative of the Kathryn Kuhlman Foundation. "Benny, I know you have wanted to meet Kathryn for some time and I have it all arranged. In fact I have been telling her about your ministry. Can you be in Pittsburgh next Friday morning? She will be able to meet with you right after the service."

"Of course. I'll be there!" I replied with great excitement.

The idea that I would finally have the opportunity to meet Miss Kuhlman was thrilling. I wanted to express my gratitude for the pivotal role she had played in my life.

I arrived early at First Presbyterian Church. As usual, people were lined up by the hundreds waiting for the doors to open. A few minutes later a staff member came to me and said, "I know that you are here to meet with Miss Kuhlman after the service. However, she will not be here today. She is sick and has been taken to the hospital."

No one could remember anything like this happening before. Kathryn *never* canceled a service. A few minutes later the entire waiting crowd was given the same message. The news was cause for great concern. They were stunned. In hushed whispers they asked each other, "I wonder how serious it really is? Do you think they will tell us more?"

There was no reason for me to stay. I left Pittsburgh and returned to Canada.

It Was Meant To Be

It was only two months later that this unforgettable woman went to be with the Lord.

Many times I've been asked, "Benny, tell me about Miss Kulhman. What was she like?"

They are surprised when I tell them, "Oh, I never had the opportunity to meet Kathryn personally."

Looking back on my journey to Pittsburgh, I believe what happened that day was in God's providence.

As I told members of my staff recently, "Had I met Kathryn it is possible that I would have forever believed she gave the anointing to me, or that God may have used her in some way to transfer it to me." No, the Lord wanted me to clearly know that the anointing comes from Him, not from any person.

God uses His servants to influence us to walk in His ways — even to bring us into an atmosphere where miracles occur. The Lord did not give me any special power or gift through Kathryn Kuhlman, instead He used her to help me *find* the anointing. As you will read in these pages, God certainly uses people, but He is your only Source.

Why do I want to share this remarkable story of Kathryn Kuhlman with you? It demonstrates what can happen when an ordinary person becomes totally yielded to the Holy Spirit.

In her lifetime she said she died one thousand deaths, yet there was great triumph. Her God was very much alive.

Chapter Two

Miracles on Main Street

"It was a phenomenon!" my friend Ralph Wilkerson told me recently. "That's the only way I can describe Kathryn's meetings at the Shrine." The founder and pastor of Melodyland Christian Center in Anaheim, California, was talking about the monthly Sunday afternoon meetings Miss Kuhlman conducted at the 7,500 seat Shrine Auditorium in Los Angeles during the final decade of her life.

"The doors didn't open until one o'clock in the afternoon," said Ralph, "but by nine-thirty in the morning the crowds were so large that special officers had to be hired to maintain order." Only those in wheelchairs or on stretchers — and there were many — were given early entrance at a designated door.

People arrived by taxis, limousines, pickup trucks and on foot. Buses and even planeloads came from major cities in the west and often from foreign countries. "It wasn't unusual for forty or fifty charter buses to arrive for a single service," recalls Ralph. On some days the building could have been easily filled twice. Thousands of disappointed people had to be turned away.

Before each service hundreds of choir members rehearsed under the direction of Dr. Arthur Metcalfe, a distinguished musician who had been with Miss Kuhlman for years. At the organ was another longtime member of the team, Charles Beebee. The ushers and counselors were at their appointed locations, while Kathryn was backstage, simultaneously praying and double-checking to make sure every detail of the service was in place.

Ten minutes from the time the doors opened, the building was packed to capacity. "Kathryn always believed that when the building was full, it was time to begin — even if it was much earlier than the announced starting time," Wilkerson told me.

Thunderous Applause

Jamie Buckingham once described the beginning of a service he attended at the Shrine. "The choir exploded into song.

'Exploded' is the only word for it as they rang out the sounds of *Pentecostal Fire*," he said. "They did not just sing, they overflowed; they erupted in joyous acclamation of sound and harmony. The music pealed until the walls fairly vibrated and my scalp tingled."

After Dr. Metcalfe led the choir in a few more stirring anthems and choruses, they began singing what became a "trademark" of Kathryn's ministry: *He Touched Me.*

It was usually during that song that Miss Kuhlman suddenly appeared on the platform. As Buckingham described it, "Her long auburn hair glistened under the bright, colored lights. Her smile was captivating, entrancing. Electricity seemed to crackle from her. The congregation burst into thunderous applause, a spontaneous demonstration of their love for her."

> "HER SMILE WAS CAPTIVATING, ENTRANCING. ELECTRICITY SEEMED TO CRACKLE FROM HER."

A Holy Hush

In every meeting, people were caught up in a genuine spirit of worship — not of Kathryn, rather the God she served. The music and praise continued until a holy hush fell across the room and she would pray — nothing memorized, but something drawn deep from within. "We know, Father, that miracles are going to happen in this place today. We feel the blessed presence of the Holy Spirit. We promise to give You all the praise, all the glory, for what is about to happen here. Pour out Your Spirit upon us, for Jesus' sake."

> HER MEETINGS WERE ALWAYS ALIVE WITH LAUGHTER. IT WAS A GENUINE REFLECTION THAT MIRRORED HER PERSONALITY.

After committing the service to the Lord, Kathryn usually entered into a light moment with her audience — perhaps something humorous that had occurred that week, or asking people to shout out the states or nations they had come from to attend the service. Her meetings were always alive and often filled with laughter. It was a genuine reflection that mirrored her personality.

It Was Powerful

People were drawn to Miss Kuhlman's meetings because of

the manifestations of the Spirit. They never knew quite what to expect. Sometimes she would preach for an hour or more. On other occasions she would invite people to the stage who had been healed in previous meetings. Often, hundreds were "slain in the spirit," something we will explore later.

Finally, there would be a moment when she felt the healing power of God begin to touch people in the audience. It was powerful. "Just a minute," she would say, pointing immediately to a spot in the balcony, "someone has just received a healing in their lower back. And somebody's vision is being restored."

The crowd would stir — looking around as Kathryn called out dozens of healings. Staff members, led by Maggie Hartner and Ruth Fisher, fanned out across the auditorium to hear firsthand accounts of miracles. Many were ushered to the platform to share their healings publicly.

The medically documented stories of the miracles that took place are recorded in her books: *God Can Do It Again, Nothing Is Impossible with God* and *I Believe in Miracles*.

The Scoffers

Were there critics? Of course there were. Historian Helen Kooiman Hosier wrote in her biography of Miss Kuhlman, "I had discovered again and again that a great majority of people began as scoffers when they visited her services. They came out of curiosity as much as anything. They were wary. There was open distrust on the part of some; desperation on the part of countless others; and still others were intensely loyal. There were extremes of reactions, but no one could get away from the fact that something out of the ordinary happened."

The Greatest Miracle

At virtually every service, Kathryn concluded with an impassioned plea for people to give their hearts to Jesus Christ. Hundreds would flock to the front, cramming the aisles to pray the sinners prayer with her. She truly believed it when she said, "Having your sins forgiven is the greatest miracle of all."

As the service concluded with the choir singing a powerful arrangement of *He's the Savior of My Soul,* Miss Kuhlman left the stage, but not the building. She immediately walked to the section filled with wheelchairs and stretchers, praying for those who had not been healed.

When people looked at their watches, they couldn't believe it. They had been in the auditorium for four hours, yet it seemed like forty minutes.

Making Headlines

In the late 1960s and early 1970s Miss Kuhlman's name

became a household word. There were four-page photo spreads in *People* magazine, she was a guest of Johnny Carson on *The Tonight Show* and appeared on the *Dinah Shore Show*. Popular comedians of the day, Flip Wilson and Ruth Buzzi, would mimic her dramatic style. Millions were glued to her weekly television program and there was standing room only in auditoriums across America.

Time magazine wrote in 1970, "Kathryn Kuhlman looks for all the world like dozens of the women in her audience. But hidden underneath the 1945 Shirley Temple hairdo is one of the most remarkable Christian

> MILLIONS WERE GLUED TO HER WEEKLY TELEVISION PROGRAM AND THERE WAS STANDING ROOM ONLY IN AUDITORIUMS ACROSS AMERICA.

Charismatics in the U.S. She is, in fact, a veritable one-woman shrine of Lourdes. In each of her recent services — in Los Angeles, Toronto and her home base of Pittsburgh — miraculous cures seem to occur."

Many are surprised to learn that her move to the national stage came after great reluctance.

In the early 1950s, Kathryn ventured to nearby cities such

as Akron and Cleveland, yet not much farther. Invitations poured in from Dallas, Seattle, Los Angeles, London and beyond — all courting her to bring her dynamic ministry to their cities. For reasons no one could understand, she turned them all down. For nearly fifteen years she was content to stay in her own backyard.

> FOR NEARLY FIFTEEN YEARS SHE WAS CONTENT TO STAY IN HER OWN BACKYARD.

"I'm Not Interested"

"I literally begged and begged Kathryn to hold meetings on the West Coast and she refused," Ralph Wilkerson told me. His own healing ministry was flourishing in Anaheim and he felt she would only multiply what God was already doing in southern California.

Ten years earlier, there had been a prophecy given by Assembly of God evangelist C. M. Ward to Wilkerson that two things were going to happen in the kingdom: "There is going to be a major reemphasis on Bible teaching and there is going to be a great woman evangelist who will come to the West

Coast." Ralph never forgot those words.

The California minister often sponsored large rallies in the area, including those featuring David Wilkerson (no relation), founder of Teen Challenge and author of *The Cross and the Switchblade*. Miss Kuhlman had been a strong financial supporter of the Teen Challenge drug rehabilitation projects and David repeatedly urged Ralph to invite her.

"I told Dave that if he would help to arrange a meeting with Kathryn, my wife and I would gladly fly to Pittsburgh," says Ralph. "I had never been in one of her services and was anxious to meet her personally."

Even with all the glowing reports, Ralph Wilkerson wanted to make certain this was the type of ministry he could endorse. The meeting was arranged and, in the late summer of 1964, Ralph and his wife, Allene, boarded a plane for Pittsburgh.

An Unmistakable Presence

They knew that Kathryn conducted a weekly Sunday morning meeting in Youngstown, Ohio, just across the state line from Pennsylvania. Unannounced, they drove to the Stambaugh Auditorium and slipped into the service. "We arrived an hour early and could hardly find a place to sit in the 2,500 seat building," recalls Ralph.

The moment Kathryn walked onto the platform they felt the unmistakable presence of the Lord. "We were totally at home. The music, the message, the miracles, the freedom in the Spirit — it was much like the services we were conducting in Anaheim." Ralph was convinced this woman of God would have a mighty impact on southern California.

The next morning, before their scheduled meeting with Miss Kuhlman at her Carlton House offices, Ralph walked the streets of downtown Pittsburgh, questioning people about her ministry. "I did not encounter one person who didn't know about her — and even though most were not her followers, they spoke in glowing terms of her work in their city." He heard stories about alcoholics who were now singing in her choir, and met one man whose wife was healed in her service.

"Why Should I Come?"

That afternoon Ralph and Allene poured out their hearts to Kathryn. They shared the vision they had for Los Angeles. "I'm sure this is of God," Ralph confided in her.

"Why should I come?" she replied, talking about the full

schedule of ministry she had in Pennsylvania and Ohio. She also laughed about being a country girl from Missouri and wondered whether she'd be accepted in the movie capital of the world. Politely, but firmly, she told the Wilkersons, "No, I'm really not interested."

"Please pray about it," pleaded Ralph before they left. "Please pray."

"Keep Asking"

Months went by. There was no response from Miss Kuhlman.

Then one day in early 1965 the telephone rang. "Hello. Is this Allene?" asked the voice on the other end of the line. "This is Oral Roberts."

> SHE LAUGHED ABOUT BEING A COUNTRY GIRL FROM MISSOURI AND WONDERED WHETHER SHE'D BE ACCEPTED IN THE MOVIE CAPITAL OF THE WORLD.

Oral was a good friend of the Wilkersons; they had helped him in many of his crusades through the years. Oral explained that he was in a crusade in Cleveland, Ohio, and the mother of his organist had just passed away. "I know this is short notice, but can you possibly come and fill in for her?"

Allene talked it over with Ralph and he told her, "You can go on one condition."

"What's that?" she asked.

> ## "DON'T LEAVE UNTIL SHE AGREES TO COME TO SOUTHERN CALIFORNIA."

"After the crusade I want you to travel on to Pittsburgh and see Kathryn Kuhlman again. And don't leave until she agrees to come to southern California."

Not only did Allene arrange to meet with Kathryn, but she was invited to stay at her home in Fox Chapel, a suburb on the north side of the Allegheny River.

"Ralph, I'm doing my best to encourage her to come west, but she still refuses," Allene told her husband when she called home the first night. "Well, please keep asking," he insisted.

Miss Kuhlman talked about her overwhelming workload. "I really don't want to expand this ministry," she explained.

Allene was determined. Then, on the fourth day, Kathryn took her aside and told her, "I've been praying about this and I really do think this is of God. Tell Ralph I'll come to California, but only for one meeting. Only one!"

Ralph immediately booked the Civic Center in Pasadena and 2,500 attended — most from Wilkerson's church since

Miss Kuhlman was hardly known on the West Coast.

"The news of the miracles in that service spread like wildfire." recalls Ralph. "Kathryn forgot about her 'just one service' agreement and returned a month later for a second meeting."

Capturing the City

By the third service the Civic Auditorium was packed to the rafters and disappointed hundreds could not get in.

Within a few months it was obvious that Kathryn needed a much larger building. "Charter buses were arriving for the services," remembers Ralph.

Miss Kuhlman negotiated with the owners of the 7,500 seat Shrine Auditorium, off the Harbor Freeway near downtown Los Angeles. Jammed to capacity, more than 2,000 were turned away the first Sunday afternoon. This story would be repeated for the next ten eventful years.

She captured the city. "Once, during a book signing at the May Company department store, the lines waiting to greet Miss Kuhlman were out the door and snaked around the block," Wilkerson told me.

On the Set

Her monthly visits to California, the heart of the world's

largest film and television production studios, sparked her interest in the possibility of adding media to her ministry outreach. There was a problem, however. She wouldn't even consider such a venture unless she could find the best producer and the finest studio available. Everything she did for the Lord had to be done first class. Those who know me know that I agree with this philosophy and make no apology for expecting excellence. Many times I've looked into the faces of my staff and said, "Remember, the Lord deserves our best."

In the spring of 1966 she was introduced to Dick Ross, a producer who was highly respected in Hollywood's motion picture industry. He had just completed fourteen years of producing widely acclaimed films for the Billy Graham organization.

Their personalities clicked the first time they met at the Century Plaza Hotel where Miss Kuhlman stayed during her trips to Los Angeles. They decided on a weekly half-hour format with the title "I Believe in Miracles," and signed a contract to produce the series at CBS Studios.

The set was a garden adorned with flowers. There was music, an interview with someone who had been healed by the Lord through her ministry and a heart-to-heart talk. Simple, yet effective.

Each second month, on a Wednesday and Thursday,

Kathryn would tape eight programs — she didn't believe in reruns. With 500 programs in just under ten years it became the longest running half-hour series ever produced at CBS. It was syndicated in major markets across the nation.

> WITH 500 PROGRAMS IN JUST UNDER TEN YEARS, IT BECAME THE LONGEST RUNNING HALF-HOUR SERIES EVER PRODUCED AT CBS.

Those who worked with her say that after each taping she immediately went into a private viewing room and critically watched every segment. If there was the slightest error, she would come back into the studio and ask for a retake.

"Queen of the Lot"

Dick Ross told one reporter, "Right from the start Kathryn Kuhlman was accepted by the CBS staff and became sort of a queen of the lot. When she'd come into the studio there was a constant procession of people from the executive level on down — people who loved her — who would stop by just to see her and say hello."

Often, a cameraman or an individual from the editing booth

would bring a sick child or family member and ask Kathryn to pray for them. She never refused.

As Miss Kuhlman left the studio, she'd often hear CBS staffers who rarely darkened the door of a church say, "I'll be at the Shrine next month." Ross observed, "Television became her medium. It went hand in glove with her platform services. The services were where the miracles happened; the television series became the means of sharing with millions across the country."

> "THE SERVICES WERE WHERE THE MIRACLES HAPPENED, THE TELEVISION SERIES BECAME THE MEANS OF SHARING WITH MILLIONS ACROSS THE COUNTRY."

"Why Not?"

Kathryn had a delightful sense of humor.

Jimmie McDonald, who has sung at many of our crusades, recalls the day one of the floor directors at CBS wanted to play a prank on Carol Burnett, who also taped her show at the studios. "When she heard of the plot," says Jimmie, "Kathryn got that little girlish look in her eyes and smiled. 'Yeah. Why not?'"

The man explained that Carol Burnett boasted to her co-stars that she always knew what was going on during her show, and she held the record for not being "broken up" by anybody. The floor director told Kathryn, "Carol is supposed to say her line and open the door. And one of her costars is expected to come out and surprise her — but it will be you! We'll see then if we can finally break her up."

Says McDonald, "Kathryn thought this would be extremely funny and agreed to do it. She crept into the next-door studio and stood waiting out of sight. On cue she rapped at the set door. When Carol Burnett called for the person to come out, Miss Kuhlman walked through the door and onto the set. She exclaimed, 'Have you been waaaaiting for me?'"

Adds Jimmie, "Carol Burnett finally lost it, and collapsed to the floor, laughing uncontrollably. It was payback time for the many times Carol brought down the house with her over-the-top Kathryn Kuhlman imitations." No one is sure if the clip ever aired, but it certainly became the talk of CBS studios.

A long list of show business celebrities attended her meetings at the Shrine Auditorium. A section in the balcony was reserved where they could slip in and not be bothered — and Kathryn made it a policy never to single them out from the platform.

Letter from the Mayor

Because of the growing national television exposure, Miss Kuhlman received hundreds of invitations from around the globe — from churches of many denominations, seminaries, international conferences and conventions.

One letter immediately caught her attention. It was from Oran Gragson, the Mayor of Las Vegas, Nevada, and the entire City Council. They were extending an official invitation for Miss Kuhlman to visit their city. Even more, they promised to do everything in their power to make the event a great success.

> ONE LETTER IMMEDIATELY CAUGHT HER ATTENTION. IT WAS FROM ORAN GRAGSON, THE MAYOR OF LAS VEGAS, NEVADA.

Her mind began to whirl. Not only would she accept the invitation, she would have the entire service filmed! That would be quite a departure from the norm.

Kathryn constantly refused to allow video or motion picture cameras to be present at her services. She felt the activity would distract her from concentrating on what God wanted to take place. Only four times did she make an exception. Ralph Wilkerson was permitted to videotape her ministry at a charismatic conference at Melodyland in 1969, videos were made when she spoke at the 1974 and 1975 World Conferences on the Holy Spirit in Israel, and the entire Las Vegas miracle service.

What made her decide to capture the Las Vegas event on film? One of her close friends told me, "I believe Kathryn knew the seriousness of her physical condition and believed the time had come for one of her services to be preserved for all time. Of course, she wanted it done with great perfection."

Kathryn also knew that if anyone could produce the quality film she had in mind it was Dick Ross, the director of her television program.

The City was Buzzing

As preparations neared for the service at the Convention Center, Mayor Gragson proclaimed May 3, 1975, "Kathryn Kuhlman Day in Las Vegas." The entire city was buzzing about it. Posters advertising the meeting were seen in gambling casinos and announcements were made in nightclubs. It's recorded that, "A Jewish comedian, headlining a show at the Circus Maximus, a plush supper club at Caesar's Palace, jabbed his cigar at the packed audience and said, 'Oh, by the way,

Kathryn Kuhlman's in town. You know who she is, don't you? The mayor has invited her to hold a miracle service in the City Auditorium. I hope you can tear yourselves away from the slot machines to attend. I'll be there. That Kathryn Kuhlman, she's quite a gal!'"

Ministers from dozens of local churches had their members working and praying for weeks prior to the event. And a priest at one of the largest Roman Catholic churches in the area held a special Mass the day prior to the service.

The night before the meeting the casino hotels in what is often called "Sin City" were filling up — the Stardust, the Sahara, the Hilton — not with gamblers, but with God's people. They had come from nearly every point on the compass.

The scene outside the Convention Center the next morning was chaotic. Busloads began arriving from Reno, Phoenix, San Francisco and other cities. There were charter flights from Denver, Dallas, St. Louis, and Seattle. Even a group from Hawaii.

Eight thousand packed the Convention Center and thousands more were unable to gain admittance.

A reporter for *Logos Journal* (July 1975) wrote, "They were all there. The casino operators. The prostitutes. The gamblers. The entertainers. The chorus girls. The strippers.

The black jack dealers. Plus the Christian community who had worked so hard prior to her arrival. And the mayor was on the front row."

Oh what a service it was! I have watched the film dozens of times and never fail to feel the anointing of the Holy Spirit that permeated that place.

Over 700 in the choir lifted their voices, accompanied by a full orchestra. Jimmie McDonald sang as never before. And when Kathryn walked on that stage the applause was deafening.

> I HAVE WATCHED THE FILM DOZENS OF TIMES AND NEVER FAIL TO FEEL THE ANOINTING OF THE HOLY SPIRIT THAT PERMEATED THAT PLACE.

She prayed that day, "Wonderful Jesus, I don't have a thing. But if You can take nothing and use it, I offer You that nothing. I know I love You; all I can give You is my life and every ounce of strength in my body. That's all I can give."

Now He Could Hear!

Faith began to build when Kathryn invited Sunny Simons

to the microphone. She was a chorus girl who told of her miraculous healing of multiple sclerosis at a meeting in Los Angeles.

In the middle of the service healings began taking place in every section of the Convention Center and people were running to the front to give their testimonies, including an agnostic who had been deaf in both ears. Now he could hear!

> HER MESSAGE THAT DAY ON THE LORDSHIP OF CHRIST WAS STRAIGHT-FORWARD AND UNCOMPROMISING.

Her message that day on the Lordship of Christ was straight-forward and uncompromising. "Do you want the wonderful assurance of salvation? Wouldn't you like to know your sins have been forgiven?"

It was impossible to tally the number who came forward for salvation. The front of the auditorium became a mass of humanity.

Jimmie McDonald began to sing, "Allelujah, Allelujah," and the entire audience joined him in raptured praise — including a uniformed security guard who had tears streaming down his face. It was a fitting climax for an historic film that would bear the title: *Dry Land, Living Water.*

Kathryn ministered that day for nearly five hours. Las Vegas may have been the host for many spectacular events, yet it had never witnessed anything like this.

Following that day, Miss Kuhlman became more keenly aware that the clock was ticking on her life. In the months ahead there would be valleys and victory, triumphs and tragedy. However, none of this was new. It was the continuing saga of her captivating life.

Let me take you on a journey to the place it all began.

Chapter Three

"Can't You Be Quiet?"

It was a sweltering summer morning as we drove east on Interstate 40 from Kansas City. "I hope you realize how much this journey means to me," I told the friends in the car. That same night, Thursday, July 15, 1993, we would begin a two night crusade at Kemper Arena, yet this fifty-five mile drive through the rolling farmlands of western Missouri was more than a side trip. To me it was a pilgrimage.

We turned right on State Road 23 and immediately saw a sign welcoming us to Concordia — the village Kathryn

Kuhlman had called home for the first fourteen years of her life.

Down at Topsy's Cafe we had a neighborly conversation with Willis Oglesby, the mayor of this German Lutheran community of just over two thousand residents. "We're proud of our little town," he smiled, bragging about its century-old history, "but I guess we're best known around the country as the birthplace of Miss Kuhlman."

> SAUERKRAUT, BRATWURST, GERMAN POTATO SALAD, FRESH TOMATOES, AND HOMEMADE PIES.

That same week buses carrying a tour group of 150 from St. Louis arrived. Their pre-planned excursion included visiting the childhood sites of Kathryn, then a catered lunch by Saint Paul's Lutheran High Booster Club — sauerkraut, bratwurst, German potato salad, fresh tomatoes, and homemade pies.

Hearts in Harmony

During my visit there I learned that the first wave of immigrants began tilling this soil-rich land in 1839 and sought to build a community based on hard work, mutual respect and brotherly love. When their numbers grew and it was time to give their new home an official name, the settlers wanted it to reflect their unity or *concord*. The town logo mirrors those sentiments. It includes three intertwined hearts with the words "Concordia, Hearts in Harmony since 1860."

Kathryn's grandparents, John Henry Kuhlman and Catherine (Borgstedt) were married in Germany and were fascinated with the stories of those who had crossed the Atlantic to settle in a place called Missouri. In 1853 they boarded a ship and began their American adventure.

Four miles south of Concordia, the couple located 160 acres that seemed to have potential. At that time the government was selling plots for about $1.25 an acre.

After months of chopping, tilling, sawing, and building, they created the Kuhlman family farm.

Their dream of living in a land of peace was shattered nine years later when Missouri, a slave state, was caught up in the Civil War. Many of the wealthy landowners in nearby Lexington had slaves, but not the Germans of Concordia. In 1862 and 1863 lawless bands of Confederate sympathizers called "Bushwhackers" conducted savage raids on their town. Innocent citizens were killed and mutilated. Families were tied to their beds as their homes were burned to the ground. A marker near City Hall honors the Concordians who died at the hands of these treacherous men.

Not long after those frightening days, on April 11, 1865, the Kuhlmans welcomed their seventh child, Joseph, to the family homestead. Of course, no one could have imagined that Joe would become the father of someone who would one day be called, "the most prominent woman evangelist who ever lived."

"The Colonel"

Joe was twenty-five when he married seventeen-year-old Emma Walkenhorst, daughter of one of the town's community leaders. Her father, William, served in six battles of the Civil War and became the postmaster. Well respected, the townspeople called him "The Colonel."

Although Missouri didn't issue birth certificates until 1910 and copies of the local newspaper are missing from 1907 to 1911, local school documents and an old family Bible record that Kathryn Johanna Kuhlman was born on May 9, 1907. She was Joe and Emma's third child. Myrtle, her older sister, was fifteen at the time, and her brother, Earl, was ten. Later, a baby girl named Geneva completed the family.

Miss Kuhlman was often coy when people wanted to know

the actual date of her birth. I guess it's a woman's prerogative to want to appear younger than she really is.

Joe ran a successful dray business, owning carts built for carrying heavy loads that were pulled by teams of horses. In addition to his delivery company he also owned a livery stable. Through the years he became an influential citizen and was elected mayor of the city.

Kathryn was two years old when her father sold the farm and built "the big white house in town" he had always promised Emma. I enjoyed visiting the attractive two-story home at 1018 St. Louis street.

I chatted with Roland Petering, one of Kathryn's childhood chums who was raised in the house next door. "What was she like as a kid?" I asked him.

> "OH, SHE WAS ALWAYS FULL OF MISCHIEF," HE SMILED.

"Oh, she was always full of mischief," he smiled.

Petering moved to Kansas City, yet never lost touch with his Concordia playmate. "She always sent me signed copies of her latest books and when I visited one of her meetings she called me up to the stage," he recalled. They laughed publicly about the mud pies they used to make as children.

A Surprise for Mama

Remembering her early days, Kathryn particularly enjoyed relating the story of how she once surprised her mother. "I wasn't yet six, but I thought it would be the most wonderful thing in the world to give Mama a surprise birthday party. I wanted to please her so. Without telling anybody in my family, I went around the town and invited all the ladies who had been nice to me."

> "I THOUGHT IT WOULD BE THE MOST WONDERFUL THING IN THE WORLD TO GIVE MAMA A SURPRISE BIRTHDAY PARTY."

She visited each one and announced, "Now Monday is my mama's birthday and I want you come to our house at two o'clock and bring a cake."

Kathryn explained, "You see it was Mama's theology that rain or shine we washed on Mondays. Always. It was washday." That's when she would bring out the old washboard, the galvanized tub and the hand wringer.

Monday arrived, and after Emma finished the weekly wash she took a little nap. At two o'clock sharp the doorbell rang. "Mama, in her curlers and wearing a soiled work dress, came to the front door. And there was a woman she would never have let in her house, standing on the porch with a cake." More of the invited guests were arriving right behind her, dressed in their Sunday best — each one with a beautifully decorated cake.

Kathryn's mother was completely embarrassed and wanted to run and hide. She couldn't; they had seen her. Emma had no other option than to let the women in. "Happy Birthday!" they all exclaimed. A delighted Kathryn watched the proceedings from behind the bushes. "I invited thirty and they all showed up."

Emma survived the surprise. However, Kathryn was in big trouble. "For the next two weeks I ate my breakfast, lunch, and dinner standing up," she recalled.

"You're Expelled!"

The outgoing redhead could talk people into almost anything. One prank, however, backfired. Once she persuaded some fellow students into attending a funeral at the Evangelical church. None of them had the slightest idea who had passed away, but they decided to act as if they did. How did she pull off such a stunt? "I convinced the kids we could make the dead happy. It was contributing to humanity."

The escapade wasn't received well by school officials. Their judgment was harsh. "You're expelled!" they told her. It took some earnest pleading from her father before she was reinstated at her desk.

> HER FREQUENT
> CHASTISEMENTS
> DIDN'T DAMPEN
> HER SPIRIT OF
> ADVENTURE.

Her frequent chastisements didn't dampen her spirit of adventure.

Historian Wayne Warner relates, "A favorite memory for Kathryn in Concordia was the annual street fair, or Fall Festival, which is still a highlight every September. The rides, the cotton candy, the freaks of nature and other wonders made the festival the event of the year. One fair, however, was traumatic because it involved the death of Kathryn's pet rooster."

Kathryn said, "I decided I would enter my banty rooster in the poultry competition." Without a word to her family, she put the rooster into a box and placed it in her wagon. "I knew I would get a blue ribbon."

It didn't happen. As she was pulling her precious cargo

across the street, something dreadful took place. Said Kathryn, "An old farmer driving horses and a wagon was coming down the street, and the horses got scared."

Continues Warner, "The horses bolted and Kathryn ran to get out of their way, leaving her banty rooster in the middle of the street. In the melee that followed, the horses pulled the wagon over Kathryn's wagon, crushing her banty rooster."

Those who remember these early days talk about her outgoing personality rather than her study habits. Even she admitted the same: "My grades were not great, but I made people happy."

Her flair for the dramatic was evident at an early age. When there was a school party, it was always Kathryn who took charge and organized the entertainment.

"Start Scrubbing!"

Hard work ran in the Kuhlman family. She often said, "In Concordia, Missouri, if you got up in the morning and you didn't feel good, do you know what those German Lutheran folk did? They went out and worked."

Kathryn recalled that once when she wasn't feeling well, her mother said, "That's all right, honey. You just take the scrub brush, and you start scrubbing the sidewalks. It won't be long until you'll feel better."

"I Knew His Tenderness"

Joe Kuhlman was a tall man with curly hair and a mustache. Kathryn absolutely adored her father. She told one audience, "If you know me well, you know that of all human beings I have known, my relationship with Papa was the greatest. Oh! I would hang on him. I would love him. As soon as he came home and hung up his coat — before he ever had a chance to wash his hands and comb his hair — I would be hanging on him. He would sit down to rest a minute and I was all over him, my arms around his neck, yakking, chatting, never shutting my mouth, my words coming so fast."

> HER MOTHER WOULD SCOLD KATHRYN AND SAY, "CAN'T YOU BE QUIET? PAPA'S TIRED. JUST SIT DOWN AND BE QUIET."

Her mother would scold Kathryn and say, "Can't you be quiet? Papa's tired. Just sit down and be quiet."

Kathryn often said she could not remember her father punishing her. "He never laid his hands on me. Never. Not once!"

In one of her meetings she recalled, "There are many who never understood the tenderness of Joe Kuhlman's heart. They knew Joe Kuhlman as a man, one who held political office, or simply as a man of strong character, one who was dependable. Everyone in Concordia, Missouri, knew Joe Kuhlman. Perhaps each had a different idea of him."

She continued, "But I knew a different Joe Kuhlman, different from any other person's concept. I knew his tenderness when I, as a little girl, suffered with terrific ear-aches. The memory of that pain has stayed with me all my life. But I can remember how Papa would hold me tenderly in his arms. There was something — a tenderness about laying my head on Papa's shoulder — that brought relief to my suffering, there was something there that I could never describe."

Kathryn wished she could relate such stories about her mother, but their relationship was just the opposite. "Mama was the disciplinarian," she stated. "I got it down in the basement so the neighbors could not hear me scream."

Papa Was a Baptist

Miss Kuhlman came by her ecumenical leanings naturally. She was raised in a Lutheran community by a Baptist father and a Methodist mother.

Joe called himself a Baptist and his name was entered on the membership rolls, yet, as Kathryn remarked, "My papa never overworked this thing of going to church, and I'm putting it mildly."

> "IF HE SAW A PREACHER COMING DOWN THE STREET IN CONCORDIA, HE WOULD WALK ACROSS THE STREET TO KEEP FROM SPEAKING TO HIM."

She once said, "I was not brought up in a deeply religious home. Not really. In fact my father had an aversion to preachers. If he saw a preacher coming down the street in Concordia, he would walk across the street to keep from speaking to him."

On her mother's side, the story differed. Emma came from a long line of ardent Methodists. Said Miss Kuhlman, "Grandpa Walkenhorst was of the firm conviction that the only folk that would make heaven would be Methodist." Then she added, "But he didn't know anything about being born again."

After marriage, Emma, being a dutiful wife, transferred her membership to the Baptist church, yet it didn't stop her from regularly attending the congregation of her youth. Every Sunday morning she dressed up the Kuhlman children and marched them to Sunday school and morning service — at the Methodist church.

Recalled Kathryn, "The only time Papa ever entered that church was Christmas when I would give my recitation. And as far as I was concerned, when I gave that recitation, the only person present was my papa."

"Please, Don't Cry"

More than once I heard Kathryn tell about an experience she called "The greatest day in my life."

"I was standing behind Mama, and the hands of the church clock were pointing to five minutes before twelve o'clock noon," she said. "I can't remember the minister's name or even one word of his sermon, but something happened to me. It's as real to me right now as it was then."

> "I WAS STANDING BEHIND MAMA, AND THE HANDS OF THE CLOCK WERE POINTING TO FIVE MINUTES BEFORE TWELVE O'CLOCK NOON."

Kathryn vividly remembered what took place as they were singing the last song. "Suddenly, I began to tremble to the extent that I could no longer hold the hymnal, so I laid it on the pew. This was my first experience with the power of God. I sat down in the pew and sobbed. I was feeling the weight of condemnation and I realized that I was a sinner. I felt like the meanest, lowest person in the whole world. Yet I was only a fourteen-year-old girl."

She explained, "Altar calls were never given in that little Methodist church. I had often seen them take in new church members, but this was much different for me. I did the only thing that I knew to do: I slipped out from where I was standing and walked to the front pew and sat down in the corner of the pew and wept. Oh, how I wept!"

Next, "A dear old lady, Martha Johannssen, a cripple who was considered 'too religious' because she had actually voiced her convictions regarding a literal hell, slipped to my side and I remember her whispering so tenderly, 'Don't cry, Kathryn. You've always been such a good girl.' Then she very gently slipped her handkerchief into my hand."

Whenever Kathryn related the details of that moment she always smiled and added, "We both knew that wasn't quite the truth. I was one of the most mischievous kids in town!"

"I remember turning to Martha Johannssen and explaining that I was crying because I had just become the happiest person in the whole world. The heavy weight had lifted. I experienced something that has never left me. I had been born again. In that moment the blood of Jesus Christ, God's Son, cleansed me from all sin."

Said Miss Kuhlman, "I had never seen anyone converted in that church. An altar call had never been given prior to my experience." The term "born again" was foreign to her.

No one fully comprehended what was taking place in the heart of this freckle-faced teenage girl. "The preacher didn't come near me. He didn't know what to do with me."

For Kathryn, walking home from church that Sunday morning was like seeing the world for the first time. "Everything looked brighter, more beautiful. I was sure Mr. Kroencke had gotten a new paint job on his house. But the house hadn't changed. Concordia hadn't changed. Kathryn Kuhlman *had* changed."

> NO ONE FULLY COMPREHENDED WHAT WAS TAKING PLACE IN THE HEART OF THIS FRECKLE-FACED TEENAGE GIRL.

She wondered if her feet even touched the ground. "My heart was light as a feather and I knew why — Jesus had come into my heart. There was no doubt in my mind after that. I knew that I knew that I knew. That was surely the beginning of everything."

> KATHRYN SKIPPED INTO THE HOUSE AND, BURSTING WITH EXCITEMENT, SAID, "PAPA, SOMETHING'S HAPPENED TO ME. JESUS HAS COME INTO MY HEART."

Kathryn skipped into the house and, bursting with excitement, said, "Papa, something's happened to me. Jesus has come into my heart."

She was not sure he really understood. "He just looked at me and said, 'Baby, I'm glad. I'm glad.' But it was surely the beginning of something that changed my whole life."

"How I Had Changed"

I'm told that a half-century later Kathryn returned to Concordia with some members of her staff. "Oh, you must see where I first accepted Jesus," she excitedly told them.

76

"I was so shocked when I found out how small that little Methodist church had gotten through the years. There was a time when it looked so big to me, it looked almost like a cathedral. Then I realized that perhaps it doesn't seat any more than 75 or 100 people."

Kathryn walked into the little vestibule. "There was the same rope that rang the bell, announcing the time of the services. It was the same bell they always tolled when someone died in town. One ringing meant a child had died, two rings meant a middle-aged person had passed away. When an elderly person died, they rang it three times. This would cause everyone to rush to the telephone and ask the operator, 'Who died?' That's Concordia, Missouri."

> "NOTHING HAD REALLY CHANGED IN THAT LITTLE CHURCH. BUT OH, HOW I HAD CHANGED."

As she walked into the church that afternoon she noticed, "The same pews were still there, the same railing, the same pulpit. Nothing had really changed in that little church. But oh, how I had changed."

The Urge to Fly

When the time came for Kathryn to join a church she chose the denomination of her father. She declared herself a Baptist and attended the Sunday night services. The rest of the time, however, she was a Methodist. That's where you could find her on Sunday morning and in the afternoon when the youth group, "The King's Herald," met. Emma Kuhlman was their Bible teacher.

As a teenager, Kathryn was extremely restless. Her oldest sister, Myrtle had married Everett Parrott, a handsome twenty-three-year-old evangelist who came through town to preach at the Baptist Church. He was a graduate of Moody Bible Institute and they were holding tent revivals in the Northwest.

SHE WOULD LAY HER HEAD ON HER PILLOW AT NIGHT AND DREAM OF THE DAY SHE WOULD ALSO FLY AWAY.

Her older brother, Earl, was consumed with his passion for flying and talked his dad into buying an airplane for him. He was a stunt pilot and a "barnstormer" in those early days of aviation. Building race cars was his second hobby and he always entered the local competition on the Fourth of July.

What about Kathryn? As a high school sophomore she would lay her head on her pillow at night and dream of the day she could also fly away — leaving Concordia to tell the world what happened to her in that little Methodist church.

That day was fast approaching.

Chapter Four

The
Deepest Valley

"Most people around here only know Kathryn by reputation," said one of the old-timers I talked with that day in Concordia. "You know, she was only sixteen when she left town."

It was the "Roaring Twenties" and Kathryn's rambunctious personality had her parents wondering how long they would be able to handle her. Just before the summer of 1924, Myrtle, the Kuhlman's oldest daughter, took a break from the tent circuit

81

of her husband, Everett Parrott, and returned home for a short visit.

"I think it would be good for Kathryn if she came with us for a few months," Myrtle told her parents. "She'd be such a great help."

With much reluctance Joe and Emma finally agreed. At the old Concordia train station they waved "goodbye" to their daughters. Kathryn somehow knew she wouldn't be coming back.

> AT EACH NEW STOP SHE WAS THE ONE WHO WALKED THROUGH THE TOWN RINGING A HANDBELL — HERALDING THE FACT THAT A REVIVAL WAS COMING THEIR WAY.

The Parrott tent revivals were not sponsored by local churches. Everett and Myrtle just went where they felt the Lord was leading and started each crusade from scratch. Kathryn certainly didn't have a lazy summer. At each new stop she was the one who walked through the town ringing a handbell — heralding the fact that a revival was coming their way. She helped set up chairs, pass out song sheets, and played piano duets with her sister before Everett's soul-stirring message and impassioned altar call.

Every Monday was washday — now it became Kathryn's job.

Although there was much hard work, there were moments she truly loved. One of her favorite times was when her brother-in-law announced, "Now I would like Kathryn to come to the pulpit and tell you how she found Christ." She didn't simply talk. Her words were dramatic and her presentation was filled with emotion.

A Definite Call

Following one of Parrott's "repent and be saved" messages, young Kathryn began to sob. "Why aren't more coming forward? " she cried. "Why aren't more being saved?"

At that moment she felt the unmistakable call of God on her life and she knew deep in her soul the Lord was preparing her to minister the Gospel. Later she would declare, "You can say anything you want about me, as a woman, having no right to stand in the pulpit and preach the Gospel. Yet even if everybody in the world told me that, it would have no effect on me whatsoever. Why? Because my call to the ministry was just as definite as my conversion."

That fall, although Kathryn had not completed high school,

she was allowed to enroll in the Simpson Bible Institute which was operated by the Christian and Missionary Alliance denomination in Seattle. The following summer, however, she was back with the Parrotts on the "sawdust trail."

During these years in the Northwest, Kathryn was exposed to Charles S. Price, who had a powerful healing ministry in the United States and Canada. His services were accompanied by manifestations which included people being "slain in the Spirit."

Kathryn was ecstatic when Helen Gulliford, the outstanding pianist who had worked with Price, Watson Argue, and other leading evangelists of the day, joined the Parrotts' evangelistic team. She was like a third sister.

Up a Tree

After dozens of revival crusades in the Northwest, a turn of events in Boise, Idaho, thrust Kathryn into a ministry of her own.

The Parrotts had rented the Women's Club in Boise for two weeks. Just before the meeting, however, marital problems between Myrtle and Everett Parrott bubbled to the surface and the evangelist announced, "I'm going ahead to set up the tent in South Dakota. Why don't the three of you stay here and conduct the revival. Myrtle, you can do the preaching."

A few nights later, after small crowds and even smaller love offerings, it was obvious to the trio that they could not survive. Myrtle decided to close the meeting and rejoin her husband. Kathryn and Helen knew in their hearts it would be futile to follow her.

"What should we do?" twenty-one-year-old Kathryn asked Helen, who was four years her senior. "Should I go back to Concordia and you go home to Oregon?"

The dilemma they faced was bleak.

"We just have a small mission. Would you consider staying to preach?" offered a Nazarene pastor who learned of their plight.

> "WE JUST HAVE A SMALL MISSION. WOULD YOU CONSIDER STAYING TO PREACH?"

"Preach?" Kathryn had often given her testimony, but had not yet delivered a full-fledged sermon!

When the two young women arrived at the storefront building in a rough section of Boise they were quite a sight. Kathryn was wearing a puffy-sleeved yellow dress that hung down to her ankles, purchased with the last few dollars she had to her name.

"The very first sermon I preached was Zacchaeus up a tree," Kathryn later recalled. "And God knows if anybody was up a tree, I certainly was when I preached that sermon. I remember well that after the sixth sermon I honestly felt I had exhausted the Bible. I'm telling you the truth. Six sermons! I had preached on Zacchaeus, I had preached on heaven, I had preached on hell, I had preached on the love of God — and what more was there to preach about?" Later she learned that she could never exhaust the truths of God's Word.

> KATHRYN AND
> HELEN BILLED
> THEMSELVES AS
> "GOD'S GIRLS."

They traveled to Pocatello, Idaho, and received permission to hold meetings in the old Opera House that had seen better days. Kathryn and Helen billed themselves as "God's Girls." From there they went on to other small towns in Idaho like Emmett, Payette, Wilder, Meridian, and Melba.

"I used to wait until those farmers were through with their milking, their plowing, their harvesting, and when it got dark, they would file in one by one," recalled Kathryn. "I've been in every one of those little crossroads towns — every one. If the town didn't have a preacher, I offered my services."

She remembered meeting the chairman of the board of a Baptist church and coaxing him, saying, "Your church is closed anyway. You haven't anything to lose, and maybe a little to gain." He opened the building and let the girls hold meetings.

When the Kuhlman-Gulliford duo arrived in Rexburg, the only place they found available to stay was an old turkey house. Armed with mops and brooms, they cleaned it out and called it home.

Reminiscing, Kathryn later remarked, "If I had to go back to those little churches tomorrow, if I had to speak to only a handful of people, I'd work just as hard. I loved those people. I would gladly have given my life for them."

The idea of women evangelists in those days was not totally foreign. Aimee Semple McPherson was making a name for herself, blazing a trail on the revival circuit and establishing Angelus Temple in Los Angeles.

"God's Girls" preached and sang in Idaho until 1933, building a great following. More important, hundreds of names were recorded in heaven. In Twin Falls, over 2,000 jammed the sanctuary of the Methodist church the night Kathryn gave her personal testimony.

A Message of Hope

"Those were the happiest days my mom and dad could ever remember," Marjorie Ferrin told me. She was talking about the five years — starting in 1933 — her parents and grandparents helped Miss Kuhlman build the Denver Revival Tabernacle in Colorado's capital city.

Kathryn and Helen began their ministry in the Rocky Mountain state with meetings in Steamboat Springs, followed by a highly publicized six-week crusade in a rented auditorium on Main Street in Pueblo.

It was the height of the Great Depression. Unemployment was over thirty percent, thousands of banks had closed, and people were destitute. Yet Miss Kuhlman believed God's message of hope could transform lives.

> IT WAS THE HEIGHT OF THE GREAT DEPRESSION AND PEOPLE WERE DESTITUTE.

"But we only have five dollars," said Earl Hewett when Kathryn suggested that he find a meeting hall to rent in Denver. Hewett had volunteered to be the business manager for Kathryn and Helen so they could devote their full energies to ministry.

Being broke was nothing new to Miss Kuhlman. "I know you can arrange something," she insisted.

On August 27, 1933, in an empty Montgomery Ward warehouse on Champa Street, Kathryn and Helen launched a two-week Denver crusade. The first night 125 people showed up in the improvised auditorium. The second evening the number grew to 400. Before the first week ended, all 500 seats were filled and people were peering in the windows, hanging on every word.

What began as a short series of meetings was extended month after glorious month. The city began listening to her popular radio program, *Smiling Through*.

Marjorie Ferrin's grandparents, Alfred and Agnes Anderson, immediately thought of Miss Kuhlman as their pastor and were as close to her personally as anyone in the congregation. She was in their home at Thanksgiving and Christmas. Their daughters, Mildred, Lucille, and Thelma, formed the "Anderson Sisters" trio and sang in the services almost every night.

The legacy of those days still lingers. Thelma's daughter, Marjorie, married Paul Ferrin — who became Miss Kuhlman's crusade choir director and television pianist during the final year of her life.

On several occasions I've shared fellowship and ministry with the Ferrins and much of what I am sharing about

Kathryn's days in Denver comes from Marjorie's memories and the contents of her cherished scrapbook.

"Stop Running!"

"Our meetings here in Denver will be coming to a close," Miss Kuhlman announced to a stunned congregation in early 1934, five months after the services began.

A lady by the name of Ina Fooks who worked with Kathryn in those early days wrote about that service. "The announcement of her intention was met by loud protest from the people to whom she had become a beloved leader. One man jumped to his feet and pledged a substantial sum to help back the building of a tabernacle."

Others joined him and a fund was established to build "a permanent home for the work." People who loved her ministry told Kathryn, "You've got to stop running. This city needs you!"

As plans were being drawn for the new church building, the meetings moved to a larger facility that could seat 700 — an empty warehouse on Curtis Street owned by a paper company.

Kathryn certainly knew how to relate to people. In her services, instead of arriving from the side of the platform, she would make a grand entrance from the back of the auditorium.

"How are you?" "Oh, it's so nice to have you here tonight," she would greet people, warmly shaking their hand, as she made her way to the pulpit.

Miss Kuhlman was a gifted communicator. Before the message she would often tell everyday stories with which people could identify. "You know, just this morning I was up in my little room in the St. Francis Hotel. Room 416. It's such a tiny little room. Mrs. Holmquist, God love her, does the best she can. But the wallpaper is peeling off the walls and the elevator is nearly always stuck. Yet for four dollars a week it's just like heaven to me."

People loved it.

> "FOR FOUR DOLLARS A WEEK IT'S JUST LIKE HEAVEN TO ME."

"When she preached, her compassion for souls was evident," says Marge Ferrin. "My mother told me Kathryn would never, never walk away from the altar or the prayer room until the last person left."

"I'm Coming Home!"

In that same hotel, the Tuesday after Christmas, 1934, Mrs. Holmquist told Miss Kuhlman there was an urgent telephone call waiting for her. It was a friend from Concordia. "Kathryn, your father has been hurt. He's been in an accident."

"Hurt? Bad?"

"Yes," was the reply.

" Tell Papa I'm leaving right now. I'm coming home."

She talked about the events in an article which appeared in *Guideposts* in 1971.

Kathryn had purchased an old V-8 Ford. She threw a few things into the back and headed home. "Only God knows how fast I drove on those icy roads, but all I could think about was my father. Papa was waiting for me. Papa knew I was coming."

> "ONLY GOD KNOWS HOW FAST I DROVE ON THOSE ICY ROADS, BUT ALL I COULD THINK ABOUT WAS MY FATHER."

Still one hundred miles west of Kansas City, she called her Auntie Belle.

"This is Kathryn. Tell Papa I'm almost home."

"But, Kathryn, didn't they tell you? Your father was killed. He was hit by a car driven by a college student who was home for the holidays. He died almost instantly."

When she arrived, her father's body rested in an open casket in the front room of their home on St. Louis Street. She was heartbroken.

Following the services in the little Baptist church, after everyone had filed out, twenty-seven-year-old Kathryn remained. "The funeral director walked over and asked, 'Would you like to see your father before I close the casket?'"

"Suddenly I was standing at the front of the church, looking down — my eyes fixed not on Papa's face, but on his shoulder, that shoulder on which I had often leaned."

Kathryn said, "I reached over and gently put my hand on that shoulder in the casket. And as I did, something happened. All that my fingers caressed was a suit of clothes. Not just the black wool coat, but everything that box contained was simply something discarded, loved once, laid aside now. Papa wasn't there."

That morning, all she could cling to were the words of the apostle Paul, ". . . to be absent from the body and to be present with the Lord" (2 Corinthians 5:8).

Dedication Day

When Kathryn returned from the funeral, she was buoyed by the emotional support that surrounded her in Denver. She was also thrilled that the search for a permanent church location had ended. They purchased a building at the corner of West Ninth and Acoma. It had been the truck garage of a large Denver department store. After major renovations, the 2,000-seat Denver Revival Tabernacle was dedicated on May 30, 1935. Again, there was standing room only.

Services continued every night except Monday.

Kathryn's basic message was salvation, yet her pulpit included those who preached on divine healing, the baptism of the Holy Spirit and prophesy. Popular visiting speakers included Howard Rusthoi, Phil Kerr, Raymond T. Richey and occasional ministry from Myrtle and Everett Parrott. Each Saturday Helen Gulliford was in charge of "Music Night."

The 1935 Christmas letter from the church read, "The outstanding feature of the work is its entirely undenominational character. Miss Kuhlman has held fixedly to the idea that God could and would use a great evangelistic center where all are welcome."

An Unforgettable Embrace

Kathryn was nervous when she learned that her mother was coming to Denver to hear her preach — it had never happened before. As a child she had desperately sought her mother's approval and affection. "She never once told me she was proud of me or that I did well. Never once." It wasn't Emma Kuhlman's nature.

The message that night was titled, *The Power of the Holy Spirit*, a departure from the usual simple salvation message that was the hallmark of her ministry in those years. She recalled, "I don't think Mama understood one thing I said. She knew nothing about the Holy Spirit — and she didn't know much about the new birth experience."

At the conclusion of the message Kathryn invited those who had a spiritual need to meet with her in the prayer room. She quietly said, "All those who want to be born again and know the Third Person of the Trinity, the Holy Spirit, come forward. Come to the prayer room behind the pulpit. I'll be back there and so will some others. We'll be praying for you."

Many people streamed toward the door that led to the special room. Talking about that night, Kathryn recalled, "When I walked off the platform, Mama was just sitting there. She didn't leave her seat."

After about fifteen minutes Kathryn saw the door of the prayer room open. "There must have been more than a hundred in there praying — everyone with their heads down — and I saw Mama come through that door."

Recalling that moment, "If you only knew my Mama. You

could not have convinced her of spiritual things. She was so set in her way. If the Methodists didn't believe it, then it wasn't so."

To Kathryn's surprise, her mother knelt down. "She hadn't been on her knees long when I slowly walked over to her. Everybody was praying. She was such a quiet woman."

When her daughter was close enough, Emma said, "I'm here because you spoke truth tonight. And I want to know Jesus as you know Him."

The moment she laid her hands on her mother's head, Emma began to tremble and cry — the same trembling and tears Kathryn had experienced in that little Concordia sanctuary. "And when I touched her, my mama began to speak in a heavenly language."

Kathryn was dumbfounded. "My mother didn't know there was such a thing as speaking in an unknown tongue. She had never read it. She had no light on it. She was not seeking for it. And Mama began speaking softly and beautifully. It was glorious."

When the Spirit had subsided, Emma Kuhlman did something that caused tears to well in the eyes of her daughter. She extended her arms toward Kathryn and embraced her. It was the first time she ever remembered being tenderly held by her mother.

Kathryn Kuhlman
building the Denver
Revival Tabernacle,
1935.

Miss Kuhlman at
First Presbyterian
Church, Pittsburgh,
Pennsylvania (left),
and at Franklin, PA,
in the late 1940s
(below).

"Kathryn Kuhlman
Day," in Las Vegas,
May 3, 1975,
(right), and at
Oral Roberts
University,
1974 (below).

Today, the ministry of Benny Hinn reaches
millions worldwide through television and crusades.

"She took both of my hands in hers and said, 'Kathryn, preach it! That others may receive what I have received.' It was the first time she had ever approved of me being in the work I was in."

Kathryn also loved to relate what transpired next. "You want to know something? My mother did not sleep for three days and two nights. So great was the joy of the Lord upon her, she couldn't sleep! And

> I HAD A NEW MAMA. SHE WAS A NEW PERSON! LOVE RADIATED FROM HER.

my mother was never the same again. I had a new mama. She was a new person! Love radiated from her. Nobody had to prompt her. Nobody had to teach her."

Until the day Emma Kuhlman went to be with the Lord in 1958, she reflected the transformation produced by the Holy Spirit.

It Was Unthinkable

Over the years, dozens of ministers were guests in the pulpit at Denver Revival Tabernacle. One of the favorites was a dynamic evangelist from Austin, Texas — Burroughs A. Waltrip. He returned again and again.

And when the evangelist settled in Mason City, Iowa, to build a 700-seat evangelistic center called Radio Chapel, Kathryn became a frequent guest preacher.

The relationship became more than ministerial. Kathryn Kuhlman fell in love. When word began to spread that she was considering marriage to this man, it was unthinkable. After all, Burroughs Waltrip was married — with a wife and two sons in Texas.

Her ardent supporters, Alfred and Agnes Anderson, drove the 800 miles to Mason City and pleaded with their beloved pastor to change her mind. They failed.

On October 15, 1938, Miss Kuhlman announced that she and Waltrip, who had divorced his wife, were combining their ministries. Their headquarters would be Mason City and she and Waltrip would alternate commuting to Denver for Sunday services.

Three days later they were married at Radio Chapel in Mason City.

The congregation in Denver rejected her attempt to return in any capacity. They believed she was out of God's will.

Helen Gulliford resigned from Kathryn's ministry. In a matter of only a few weeks the flock in Denver had scattered. They were like sheep without a shepherd.

Just one year earlier, in a printed program commemorating

the "Fourth Annual Jubilee" of her ministry in Denver, Kathryn
Kuhlman included words of a message she titled, *Heartaches.*

"Sooner or later all our feet must go down that vale of
sorrow and suffering and darkness and tears," she wrote. "The
heart that has never known sorrow is dwarfed; and the nature,
which was capable of the highest heights and the deepest
depths, is undeveloped; and that life can never experience the
deepest chords of joy without having known the depths of true
sorrow."

The words were prophetic.

Kathryn Kuhlman had entered the deepest, darkest valley of
her life.

Chapter Five

Out of the
Wilderness

From the moment Kathryn married Burroughs Waltrip, the man she called "Mister," she knew it was a tragic mistake, yet there was no turning back.

The few friends who traveled from Denver to attend meetings in Mason City were troubled. The woman who had once been so exuberant and dynamic was now subdued. I'm told that one returned, saying, "All Kathryn does is sit on the platform behind her husband and cry."

Only seven months after their marriage, in May, 1939, the

local newspaper announced that Radio Chapel was in bankruptcy. The Waltrips quickly left Iowa and became itinerant evangelists — a life both of them had known so well. They labored in small churches and revival centers in Georgia, Arizona, and Pennsylvania.

The Pain of Dying

As World War II erupted in Europe, Kathryn was fighting her own private battles. No matter how she tried to rationalize her decision, the truth gripped her heart like a vise. Because of her own stubborn will, she had drifted from God's call.

The turning point of her life came on a Saturday afternoon on the outskirts of Los Angeles, several years after her misguided marriage.

In her own words, she told her friend Jamie Buckingham, "No one will ever know the pain of dying like I know it. For I loved him more than I loved life itself. And for a time I loved him more than God. I finally told him I had to leave. God had never released me from that original call. Not only did I live with him, I had to live with my conscience, and the conviction of the Holy Spirit was almost unbearable. I was tired of trying to justify myself. Tired."

Kathryn talked about the day she left their apartment and found herself walking down a shady street. "The sun was flickering through the great limbs that stretched out overhead. At the end of the block I saw a street sign. It said simply, 'Dead End.' There was heartache, heartache so great it cannot be put into words. If you think it's easy to go to the cross, it's simply because you've never been there. I know. And I had to go alone."

She confessed her transgressions to the Lord and received the assurance of God's forgiveness.

> "THERE WAS HEARTACHE, HEARTACHE SO GREAT IT CANNOT BE PUT INTO WORDS."

The Choice

Miss Kuhlman said, "I knew nothing of the power of the mighty third person of the Trinity which was available to all. I just knew it was four o'clock on Saturday afternoon and I had come to the place in my life where I was ready to give up everything — even Mister — and die."

Standing on that dead end street, Kathryn looked heavenward and cried, "Dear Jesus, I surrender all, I give it all to You.

Take my body. Take my heart. All I am is Yours. I place it in Your wonderful hands."

She admitted, "I had to make a choice. Would I serve the man I loved, or the God I loved?" She chose God.

> SHE WAS A NEW PERSON — TOUCHED BY THE POWER OF THE HOLY SPIRIT.

Three days later, on the rail platform of the Los Angeles train station, Kathryn looked at Burroughs Waltrip for the last time. She purchased a one-way ticket to the little town of Franklin, Pennsylvania, where she had been invited to speak. For her there was no turning back. The old Kathryn Kuhlman had died. She was a new person — touched by the power of the Holy Spirit.

A New Home

The Franklin Gospel Tabernacle was a rough but impressive structure in this city of ten thousand located in northwest Pennsylvania. It was built in 1929 as an interdenominational evangelistic center and had hosted prominent preachers including Billy Sunday.

Now it was in the hands of a local group of laymen who

invited evangelists to use the facility. A board member, Matthew Maloney, had somehow heard of Miss Kuhlman and asked her to hold a two-week series of meetings in May 1946.

Only thirty-eight curious townspeople showed up the first night, yet that did not bother Kathryn the slightest. The same power of the Holy Spirit she encountered on that dead end street in Los Angeles was present and she preached with a new anointing. The next night nearly 200 filed in. And soon the wood-beamed tabernacle was packed to capacity. Instead of staying two weeks, Kathryn called Franklin home for the next four years.

She began a daily radio program, *Heart to Heart*, on WKRZ in nearby Oil City. It was Denver all over again.

"Pardon Me, Miss Kuhlman"

Prior to her years in Franklin, Miss Kuhlman believed in healing and would never hesitate to pray for the sick. Yet that was not her emphasis. She was known primarily as a down-to-earth evangelistic preacher who led people to a born again experience.

In a service Kathryn conducted in Franklin, something occurred that would change the nature of her ministry forever.

"I was preaching on the Holy Spirit — the little I knew about the Holy Spirit," she recalled in one of her messages.

"Just before I began speaking, a woman stood up and I was shocked when she said, 'Pardon me, Miss Kuhlman, please — may I give a word of testimony regarding something that happened last evening while you were preaching?'"

The woman shared that during the message, "while you were telling us that in Him lay the resurrection power, I felt the power of God flow through my body. I knew instantly and definitely that I had been healed. So sure was I of this, that I went to the doctor today and he confirmed that I was healed. The tumor is gone!"

New Sight for George

The following Sunday a man named George Orr, a 76-year-old World War I veteran who had lost the sight of one eye in an industrial accident, came to the service with his entire family. He was on workmen's compensation because a number of medical doctors declared he would never again see out of his right eye — plus his left eye now had only fifteen percent vision.

In the middle of the message, "Miss Kuhlman made a statement I had never heard before," recalled George. "She said that healing was there for everyone just as salvation was." He prayed for God to touch his eyes.

Immediately, in the middle of the service, his blinded eye began to burn. By the time he reached his home, the sight had been restored to *both* of his eyes.

His healing was verified by the same doctor who had submitted the findings to the compensation board — which had resulted in state compensation for the loss of his sight.

> THE SIGHT HAD BEEN RESTORED TO *BOTH* OF HIS EYES.

George Orr's documented story is recorded in Kathryn's book *I Believe in Miracles*. She observed, "You will note that I had never prayed for George Orr; I had never touched him. His healing came to him as, unknown to me, he sat in the auditorium that May afternoon."

The Answer

Miss Kuhlman often spoke of those services. "The Holy Spirit then was the answer," she said. "An answer so profound that no human being can fathom the full extent of His depths and the full extent of His power, and yet, so simple that most folk miss it even today."

Kathryn found the answer she had been seeking. "I understood that night why there was no need for a healing line, why there is no healing virtue in a card (for a healing line) or a personality, no necessity for wild exhortations to have faith."

It was the beginning of Kathryn Kuhlman's healing ministry. She knew it was strange to some because, as she once stated, "hundreds have been healed just sitting quietly in the audience without any demonstration whatsoever. None. Very often not even a sermon is preached. There have been times when not even a song has been sung. No loud demonstration, no loud calling on God as though He were deaf. No screaming, no shouting. Within the very quietness of His presence, and there have been times, literally hundreds of times, when in the great miracle service there has been so much of the presence of the Holy Spirit that literally one could almost hear the beating, the rhythm of the heartbeat of thousands of people as their hearts did beat as one."

"Let's Buy It!"

The miracles in Franklin began to multiply. The daily radio program was added to new stations including WPGH in Pittsburgh. Crowds were arriving at the tabernacle from cities one and two hundred miles away.

In the midst of her growing ministry, legal documents for Kathryn's divorce were filed in 1947, but the topic was irrelevant. She was a new Kathryn and God had buried her past forever.

"Let's buy it!" Miss Kuhlman exclaimed when she located a skating rink in nearby Sugarcreek that could be renovated to seat 2,000 people. They named it Faith Temple. Within six months the $30,000 mortgage was paid in full.

Letters — thousands every week — were overwhelming her volunteer staff. There were heart-rending requests for prayer, miraculous testimonies of healing and an outpouring of appreciation for the way God was using Miss Kuhlman to touch their lives. And more than a few asked, "When are you coming to Pittsburgh?"

> MORE THAN A FEW ASKED, "WHEN ARE YOU COMING TO PITTSBURGH?"

The City of Steel

The thought of entering the steel-producing, predominately Catholic city was intimidating, yet Kathryn felt the time was right. She rented the 2,000-seat North Side Carnegie Music Hall for a two-week crusade starting July 4, 1948.

Historian Wayne Warner wrote, "Even that early in her

career, the building was jammed, with hundreds turned away. Some had begun to arrive at noon for the 7 P.M. service, and by 5:30 the people waiting in line were spilling out past the gaudy bars nearby. Regulars in the bars must have thought they had too much to drink when they saw the patient crowd standing in the July heat. Would a religious service draw this kind of crowd to Carnegie Hall?"

The local newspaper covered the crusade as a major event — which it truly was.

Miracles! Oh, the miracles! Goiters disappeared. Heart conditions were healed. Alcoholics were instantly delivered.

The services, and those that followed, were marked by a supernatural presence of the Holy Spirit. Kathryn said, "Many have been the times when I have felt like taking the shoes from my feet, knowing that the ground on which I stood was holy ground. Many are the times when the power of the Holy Ghost is so present in my own body that I have to struggle to remain on my feet. Many are the times when His Very Presence healed sick bodies before my eyes. My mind is so surrendered to the Spirit, that I know the exact body being healed: the sickness, the affliction, and in some instances, the very sin in their lives. And yet I could not pretend to tell you *why* or *how*."

She Didn't Understand

During these miracle meetings, scores of people Kathryn prayed for were "slain in the Spirit." They would crumple to the floor, touched by a power far greater than Miss Kuhlman. At other times people in the audience, far removed from the platform, would have the same experience.

When people questioned the biblical basis for this manifestation she would point to what happened to Saul on the road to Damascus in Acts 9. He fell to the earth under God's power.

> THEY WOULD CRUMPLE TO THE FLOOR, TOUCHED BY A POWER FAR GREATER THAN MISS KUHLMAN.

Miss Kuhlman never professed to comprehend this phenomenon. She said, "I only know that I have nothing to do with it. One of the questions I'm going to ask the Master when I get home to glory is about this manifestation of His power, the 'slaying power' of the Holy Spirit. I do not understand it."

His Knees Buckled

Kathryn particularly enjoyed telling the story of an incident that happened at her office in Pittsburgh — a story I think you'll enjoy as much as I did.

"I had just returned from lunch and was met by three men who were waiting for me," she recalled. "I recognized two of them as prominent Presbyterian ministers in the city. They introduced the third man as a professor of theology from a well-known theological seminary in the East."

One of the ministers commented, "My friend said he had heard of you and your miracle services. He wanted to stop by and meet you before leaving town."

Kathryn welcomed him and showed the man through the offices. "We went back into our recording studio where we make the tapes of our radio programs, and then I gave him copies of some of our literature." Then, as they walked back to the front offices, the professor summoned the courage to ask a question that had been bothering him.

"Miss Kuhlman, even though I teach theology, there is still a great deal I don't know about the ministry of the Holy Spirit. In particular, there is one facet of your ministry that leaves me completely baffled."

"Well, ask me. Chances are I don't understand it either," Kathryn responded.

He hesitated, then continued, "Well, it's about all this

fainting. I understand from my friends that in your meetings you often pray for people and they — they — sort of — well, faint."

"Oh, no," laughed Miss Kuhlman. "They don't faint. They simply fall under the power of God."

She gave him a brief explanation. "He smiled politely but was still obviously puzzled," she recalled. Then it was time for them to go.

Standing in the hallway, near her office door, he looked at Miss Kuhlman and said, "I may never see you again. Would you say a word of prayer for me?"

> "HE SMILED POLITELY BUT WAS STILL OBVIOUSLY PUZZLED."

As Kathryn related, "You know, I still think God has a sense of humor, for as I took a step toward him and extended my hand to place on his shoulder to pray for him, his legs suddenly buckled under him and he fell backward to the floor. I didn't even have a chance to begin my prayer with 'Dear Jesus' when suddenly he was on his back on the carpet of my office. And it was as though the whole room were filled with the glory of God."

Kathryn shook her head in amazement as both Presbyterian ministers dropped to their knees beside him. "The secretaries at their typewriters had stopped typing, and I glanced up and saw their faces bathed in tears. There was a heavenly light filling the entire office suite," she said.

The ministers helped the professor back to his feet. "He was wobbly, and staggered back a couple of steps," continued Miss Kuhlman.

One of the ministers asked, "Are you all right?"

"He stuttered for words," said Kathryn. "All he could say was 'Wheew!' And down he went again, flat on his back on the carpet. His friends helped him to his feet and he started out the door, still shaking his head with a glow on his face that must have been like the glow that was on the face of Moses when he returned from Mt. Sinai. 'Wheew!' he kept saying over and over again."

Miss Kuhlman remembered, "He was staggering, as if drunk, and he missed the door and walked into the side of the wall. The minsters grabbed him by the arms and pointed him toward the door as he wobbled out, his face still bathed in that heavenly light."

High Voltage

She offered this explanation. "All I can believe is that our spiritual beings are not wired for God's full power, and when we plug into that power, we just cannot survive it. We are wired for low voltage; God is high voltage through the Holy Spirit."

> "ALL I CAN BELIEVE IS THAT OUR SPIRITUAL BEINGS ARE NOT WIRED FOR GOD'S FULL POWER."

To Kathryn, God was not just the author of power. "He *is* power!" she would say. "Man often tries to conjure up God in his own image, shape, size and power. But God is more — far more. When we see Him or feel Him as He really is, we simply can't stand it."

She attempted to explain what takes place. "When the Holy Spirit literally comes upon a person, he cannot stand in His presence. His legs buckle. His body goes limp. Oftentimes his very soul is filled to overflowing with the Spirit Himself. It is not fainting. A person seldom loses his faculties." She added, "Usually those who go under the power are right back on their feet and testify that it was like being caught up in a giant charge of painless electricity that momentarily leaves one out of control."

The manifestation of this kind of power was present in

every Kathryn Kuhlman service until her ministry ended.

The Roof Caved In

Five months after the Pittsburgh meetings began, Carnegie Hall was still overflowing, and she preached at Faith Temple in Sugarcreek every Sunday morning. The same pattern continued for the next two and a half years.

Miss Kuhlman assembled a quality staff in Pittsburgh. She chose ushers who were both sensitive to the Holy Spirit and impeccable in their attire. Three key people who joined her in the late 1940s remained until her passing: organist Charles Beebee, pianist Jimmy Miller, and her assistant Marguerite Hartner.

I spent many hours talking with Maggie about those early Pittsburgh days. Tears would often fill her eyes as she talked about the people whose lives were touched — including her own.

Maggie told me that Kathryn was fiercely loyal to the people of Franklin. After all, they had embraced her at a critical time in her life. When the Pittsburgh staff suggested that she move her headquarters to their city, she told them, "I'll be at Faith Temple until the roof caves in."

On Thanksgiving Day, 1950, during a snowstorm, that's

exactly what happened! Eventually her entire operation was based in the Steel City.

That same month the nation became aware of Miss Kuhlman when *Redbook* magazine published an article, "Can Faith in God Heal the Sick?"

For four months a team of writers, researchers, and doctors examined eight people who claimed they had been healed in Kathryn's meetings — from a man with a broken hip to a cancer patient. The glowing, positive report converted many skeptics, including the author of the article.

Common Sense

Every one of Miss Kuhlman's services that I attended were orderly and she would halt anyone who began to shout, prophesy or speak in tongues during one of her services. To her it was an intrusion on what God was trying to do. "The Holy Spirit is a gentleman," she would say. "He does things decently and in order. When He is speaking through me, He will not interrupt

> "THE HOLY SPIRIT IS A GENTLEMAN," SHE WOULD SAY. "HE DOES THINGS DECENTLY AND IN ORDER."

Himself by speaking through someone else."

In her book *Glimpse into Glory*, she wrote, "I cannot afford to go where there is fanaticism. I have too much at stake. I have a responsibility to God." And she added, "You know, I think sometimes the world gets the idea the only people who believe in the power of God are senile women and men who are not too intelligent. All the screaming and carrying on . . . Believe me, if I was being introduced to the Holy Spirit for the very first time in a meeting like that, I'd take for the tall timbers and I'd never come back. We need an old-fashioned baptism of good common sense."

Her rules may have not been understood by some Pentecostals, yet in her meetings were Greek Orthodox, Roman Catholics, people from virtually every Protestant denomination — and those who had never darkened the door of a church. She was sensitive to their backgrounds.

Demanding the Best

The words "first class" were tied to her ministry — and she was certainly a perfectionist. Ralph Wilkerson told me, "I've never been around a person who was so concerned about detail. If one chair was out of place, she would notice it immediately."

Should a child begin to cry, an usher would move toward the mother instantly, knowing that Kathryn might stop the service if the disturbance was not halted. If a choir member wore the wrong color shirt, she would spot it in a second.

Kathryn often said, "God demands our best. And He deserves it. After all, He gave us His best when He sent His Son to earth. We must not be satisfied with giving Him less than our best in return."

> IF A CHOIR MEMBER WORE THE WRONG COLOR SHIRT, SHE WOULD SPOT IT IN A SECOND.

One of the first things I observed about Kathryn's meetings was that she was always in control. From the moment she made her appearance on the platform, she was never out of sight. While the choir sang, she stood to the side, drinking in the music. When Jimmie McDonald sang, Kathryn gave him her full attention — and people often watched her expression as much as listening to Jimmie. Without question, it was *her* meeting.

An Open Door

"Where can we go?" Kathryn wondered when she was told

that Carnegie Hall, the building she had used for nineteen years — from 1948 to 1967 — was being closed for remodeling. Her Friday morning miracle services in that auditorium had become an institution.

The answer came from Dr. Robert Lamont, pastor of the city's historic First Presbyterian Church. He had attended the 1966 World Congress on Evangelism in Berlin that resulted in a new openness toward the work of the Holy Spirit.

When some members of his church told him that Miss Kuhlman needed a new location for her Friday services, he did not close the door. After much prayer, he presented the concept to his board and they endorsed the proposal. Until her last few months on earth, Kathryn conducted her weekly services in that sanctuary. Dr. Lamont would often pray with Miss Kuhlman before she walked onto the platform.

> THOSE MEETINGS TOUCHED MY SOUL DEEPLY AND TRANSFORMED MY LIFE.

How well I remember the Friday mornings I traveled from Toronto just to be in that incredible atmosphere of the Holy Spirit. Those meetings touched my soul deeply and transformed my life.

Her ministry, as I soon learned, was far more than manifestations and miracles. She had a *message*.

Behind those flashing eyes and red hair was a person who was totally immersed in the Word.

I have often been asked, "What did Miss Kuhlman truly believe? What was at the heart of her teaching? What did she want her listeners to understand?"

Chapter Six

"I Believe! I Really Believe!"

Quietly, now quietly," Kathryn whispered into the microphone. "Everybody just be quiet."

Charles Beebee, her organist, gently lifted his foot from the pedal and played ever so softly. You could hear a pin drop at First Presbyterian.

Just seconds before, the room had been filled with stirring music and glorious praise.

As a young Christian who traveled to Pittsburgh from Canada at least once a month, this was all so new to me. It seemed like an eternity before she said again, barely audible, "He comes in when you're quiet." In hushed tones she repeated, "He comes in when you're quiet."

Like everyone in that sanctuary I waited in anticipation, wondering what would happen next.

Suddenly, in that subdued atmosphere, healings began to take place. And for the rest of the service, people moved toward the platform to confirm the wonders God had performed.

Over the next several years I witnessed scores of miracles in her services. I listened intently to every word she uttered on the subject of healing.

"My Heart Ached"

As I have studied her life, I've discovered that in the early days of Miss Kuhlman's ministry she was greatly disturbed by what she observed with those involved in the field of divine healing. She candidly remarked, "I was confused by many of the 'methods' I saw employed and disgusted with the unwise 'performances' I witnessed — none of which I could associate in any way with either the action of the Holy Spirit or, indeed, the very nature of God."

She was especially troubled when sincere people were blamed for their continued infirmities. "Too often I had seen pathetically sick people dragging their tired, weakened bodies home from a healing service, having been told they were not healed simply because of their own lack of faith," she stated. "My heart ached for these people, as I knew how they struggled, day after day. Trying desperately to obtain *more* faith, taking out that which they had, and trying to analyze it, in a hopeless effort to discover its deficiency, which was presumably keeping them from the healing power of God. And I knew the inevitability of their defeat, because they were unwittingly looking at themselves, rather than God."

The Day of Miracles

Does Jesus perform miracles of healing today? Did such miracles cease with the closing of Christ's earthly ministry?

Those were the questions Miss Kuhlman once raised in a message entitled, "The Lord's Healing Touch." "There is no

> "THERE IS NO 'DAY OF MIRACLES.'"

'day of miracles'!" she proclaimed. "Miracles are the manifestations of the power of God. This marvelous power was manifested throughout the dispensation of God the Father, throughout the dispensation of Jesus Christ the Son, and

125

continues to be manifested during this dispensation of the Holy Spirit."

How could Kathryn or anyone who experienced her meetings doubt that God was still healing today? She believed the healing work of Christ had never ceased. "Whenever God works, it is in a supernatural way; therefore miracles will continue as long as God is still on His throne," Kathryn stated. "Let me repeat: there is no 'day of miracles' with God!"

"I'm Amazed!"

"I hope you have not come to see Kathryn Kuhlman," she would say, directing the audience to take their eyes off her. "I would feel very badly if I felt you have come for that purpose. I hope you have come to meet Jesus, and to meet the Holy Spirit."

> "I HOPE YOU HAVE NOT COME TO SEE KATHRYN KUHLMAN."

To drive the point home, she would often quote the Scripture, "God hath chosen the foolish things of the world to confound the wise; and God hath chosen the weak things of the world to confound the things which are mighty . . . that no flesh should glory in his presence" (1 Corinthians 1:27,29).

She was firmly convinced that God will not share His glory with any person. "The very minute a man or a woman begins to share the glory, the power is lifted from their ministry."

Astounded by what the Holy Spirit was doing in her own meetings, Kathryn was like a wide-eyed child. "When the miracles take place . . . I am as thrilled as though I have never seen a miracle happen in all my life," she would exclaim. "I'm just as amazed as anyone else in the auditorium. Maybe more so, because I know better than anyone else that I had nothing to do with it. 'It's not by might. It's not by power, but it is by my Spirit saith the Lord.'"

There was never an illusion regarding her accountability. "I worry that sometimes people become weary of hearing me repeat, 'Kathryn Kuhlman has nothing to do with it. Kathryn Kuhlman has never healed anyone.' Yet I know the truth of that statement better than anyone else. I know it is all the supernatural power of God. My responsibility is to be very careful to give God the praise, to give God the honor, to give God all the glory."

Recognizing the treasure the Lord had imparted, she said, "I must guard that which He has given very carefully. For one day, when I stand in His glorious presence, I am going to have to give an account of that with which He has entrusted me today."

Only One Way?

Miracles took place while the service was in progress. They could happen as the choir sang, during a testimony, when the offering was being taken, or during those moments of intense quiet. To Kathryn it certainly didn't mean this was the *only* way God healed.

"If you believe that I do not acknowledge the sacramental methods of healing used in many different churches, you are under a misapprehension," she stated. "The power of the Holy Spirit is not confined to any one place or any one system."

She advised people not to become so dogmatic in their thinking, their teaching, and their methods that other truth of equal importance is excluded. As an example, she said, "We find that God gave the gift of the Holy Spirit on the Day of Pentecost and at the household of Cornelius without any human agency of 'laying on of hands'; but at the Samaritan revival (Acts 8:17) and at the Ephesus revival (Acts 19:8), the believers were filled with the Spirit by the 'laying on of hands.'"

I agree with Miss Kuhlman who believed that a person who is unyielding either way, or makes it an issue, is guilty of error.

Kathryn told the story from John 9 of how Christ healed the man who had been born blind. "In this particular instance," she said, "Jesus spat on the ground, made clay of the spittle, and He anointed the eyes of the blind man with the clay, and said unto him, 'Go, wash in the pool of Siloam . . . he went his way therefore, and washed, and came seeing.'"

She contrasted that miracle with what happened on another occasion. "As Jesus was nearing Jericho (Luke 18:35) a blind man sat along the roadside begging. In this instance we have no record whatsoever that the hand of the Master ever touched him, and we are sure no clay was put on his eyes. Jesus spoke to the man and said, 'Receive thy sight: thy faith hath saved thee' — and immediately he received his sight."

Why are these examples important? Both men were blind and both received their sight. Different methods were used in each case.

"The Miracle Lady!"

Every miracle, regardless of its magnitude, is important.

Kathryn recalled the day she was shopping at Bullock's department store on Wilshire Boulevard in Los Angeles. "I had

> EVERY MIRACLE, REGARDLESS OF ITS MAGNITUDE, IS IMPORTANT.

gone in there to get a little something, and I was walking out of the store when I saw two little boys (I found out later they were brothers) about eight and ten years of age."

The boys were standing outside the store selling candy bars.

"One came rushing up to me and said, 'Miss, would you like to buy a candy bar?' And when he looked up into my face, his eyes got big as saucers and he shouted, 'Willie! Willie! Here is the miracle lady! Here is the miracle lady!'"

Kathryn just stood there and smiled. "He was so excited, he was stuttering. 'You know, I had a miracle happen to me once. I had a wonderful miracle happen to me.'"

"What was it?" Miss Kuhlman asked.

> "GOD HAD MADE A MIRACLE FOR ME!"

"Well," he said, "one day I needed a quarter. I needed it awful bad. I asked God for a quarter. And you know what? I was walking down the street, and there on the street was a quarter! God had made a miracle for me!"

Kathryn related the incident to make this point: "To the little boy, that was a miracle," she said. "To a man who needs to be healed of cancer, finding a quarter would not be much of a miracle. The medical profession has told him there is no cure.

Then suddenly, in His tender mercy, God reaches down and the supernatural happens. Contradictory to all known scientific laws, the supernatural power of God brings healing. And that is as great a miracle as the little boy's finding a quarter on the street."

Forgetting Yourself

After years of seeing God perform miracles, Kathryn found that many times there was a "Golden Rule" principle at work — a principle which I have witnessed on many occasions in our services. People who prayed for others became personally blessed. As she explained, "Often there are those who come praying for physical healing and they get so caught up in the spiritual impact of the miracle service that they forget about their own need. They soon direct their prayers toward others and begin rejoicing over the miracles that take place. Oddly enough, it is often at this precise moment that God chooses to heal — when self is forgotten and God and others come first."

Miss Kuhlman stated that some of the greatest manifestations of His power she ever experienced happened when she realized and acknowledged her own helplessness. "You are nearest your possession of this imparted grace," she said, "when you realize your own helplessness and your complete and entire dependence upon the Lord."

Repeatedly, she expressed great concern for those who attempt to command, even *threaten* the Almighty to meet their need. "God never responds to man's demands to prove Himself. I am amazed at the number of people who try to proposition God. But you cannot put God on the spot. You cannot say to Him, 'I am not sure of You, but if You will heal me, then I will believe in You.'"

Many times Miss Kuhlman cautioned that we receive nothing by demanding of God. It is because of His great love, compassion and mercy that He gives to us. "Often we lose sight of the fact that not one of us can claim any righteousness of our own, not one is worthy of the smallest blessing. We are the receivers of His blessing because of His mercy and compassion."

> "HEALING IS THE
> SOVEREIGN ACT
> OF GOD."

After years of personally being involved in a ministry where miracles occur, I am in agreement with Miss Kuhlman when she stated this important truth: "Healing is the sovereign act of God."

Body and Soul

To Kathryn, there was an inseparable link between miracles

of the body and those of the soul. She did not believe anyone receives a physical healing without also receiving a spiritual healing. The two went hand in hand, they intertwined.

It takes place in our meetings as it happened in hers. "In every one of my miracle services," she exclaimed, "sometimes right in the middle of the service while bodies are being healed, sinners will come walking down the aisle, weeping and saying, 'I want to be born again.' Yet I have said nothing about salvation or repentance. I have given no altar call. Yet they come. It is the moving of the Holy Spirit."

It's true. When there is a mighty presence of the Holy Spirit and sick bodies are being healed, you will also find that He is touching souls. "The spiritual healing, which is the greatest of all healings, always accompanies healing miracles," said Kathryn. "In fact, that is the very reason for miracles — to glorify God and to draw men and women to Christ."

What was this "moving of the Spirit" Kathryn so often spoke of?

What did Miss Kuhlman mean when she declared, "I know the secret power of this ministry?"

Who was she referring to when she said, "Without Him I'm sunk?"

Chapter Seven

"Without Him I'm Sunk!"

"I t's her charisma!" insisted a critic who thought people were mesmerized by Kathryn Kuhlman's powerful personality. "Can't you see how she makes people laugh and cry? Look at the way she holds them in the palm of her hand. She could tell them anything and they'd believe it!"

Obviously this man did not understand that Kathryn was perhaps the most insecure person who ever stepped on a platform. Yes, she had the ability to communicate with people, but when it came to miracles she felt totally helpless. "Don't

135

you understand, people?" she would plead. "I don't have anything to lean on. Had I an education, I might have used that as a crutch. Had I talent, I might have used that as a crutch. I don't have a thing to lean on. Nothing, just Him. I know that I have no healing virtue. Believe me, without the power of the Holy Ghost I am sunk."

As she witnessed people falling under the power, being delivered and healed, she knew better than anyone else it was not the result of her ability. "I am absolutely dependent on the power of the Holy Spirit," she maintained.

Miss Kuhlman even spoke of becoming completely detached from that which transpired during a miracle service — as if she were seated with those in the auditorium watching an awesome God at work.

> "I HAVE NEVER PROFESSED TO HAVING *ANY* GIFT OF THE SPIRIT," SHE DECLARED.

When people lauded her as a woman who had the gift of faith or the gift of healing, she would stop them immediately. "I have never professed having *any* gift of the Spirit," she declared. Kathryn belived she was simply a servant, a vessel yielding her body to the Holy Spirit and that He worked through her to lift up Christ.

She believed in the gifts of the Spirit and the operation of the gifts, but was also convinced that if one has received a gift, he must not go around boasting. She exclaimed, "I get scared when someone comes around and says, 'I have the gift of so and so.'"

A heavy weight, however, rested on her shoulders. "There have been many times, with this tremendous responsibility, I wish He had called someone else instead of me," she asserted. Having been in a similar ministry for a number of years, I know what she meant.

Never a Dull Moment

Miss Kuhlman was the first Christian I ever heard who spoke of the Holy Spirit as a *person*. It was a startling revelation to me and was the catalyst that transformed my spiritual life.

"Knowing Him is exciting," Kathryn smiled. "There's never a dull moment. Never." She talked about His colorful personality, His emotions, intellect, will — all of the attributes of a real person.

I learned that you cannot put the Holy Spirit in a certain category and say, "This is how He operates." She preached that many individuals and churches attempt to limit Him, but it's impossible. "That's exactly what we are trying to do in some of our little circles — trying to put a fence around the Holy Spirit because it is our idea. It isn't long before He jumps the fence and He's gone!"

You put the Spirit in a corner and declare, "We have Him." She cautioned that one day people may wake up to find out *they* are the ones from whom He has departed. The Holy Spirit is bigger than denominational lines and greater than man's preconceived ideas.

> THE HOLY SPIRIT IS BIGGER THAN DENOMINATIONAL LINES AND GREATER THAN MAN'S PRECONCEIVED IDEAS,

"Oh, you don't know what you are missing," she frequently remarked to those who think of the Holy Spirit as simply an *influence*, or as a *mystery*. "There is just something about Him — and when you become acquainted with Him, He becomes a vital part of you and you've just started to live!"

Don't Take the Spirit

Miss Kuhlman often stated that if she knew the Holy Spirit

would depart from her, she would never again walk out on a stage, or be involved in ministry. "God can take everything that I have, I'll live on bread and water for the rest of my life, I'll preach the gospel from the street corner, *but take not Thy Holy Spirit from me.*"

Mere words could not fully express the Holy Spirit's special place in Kathryn's life or describe the fellowship she had with Him. She often spoke of a "sense of protectiveness" she felt, not wanting anyone to bring a reproach to the One who meant so much to her.

Kathryn would remind her listeners that the miracles of Jesus did not begin until He came up out of the waters of baptism and the Holy Spirit rested upon Him as a dove. The Lord also knew that every time there was a miracle, it was produced by the Holy Spirit.

"People often talk about 'my church,'" she observed, "but only Jesus could say that." She maintained that He was talking about the body of believers — then and now. And every person, whether they be Jew or Gentile, who has the new birth experience is automatically born into this body.

Kathryn preached that before Jesus went away, He wanted to give to His church — "those whom thou hast given me" (John 17:11) — the greatest gift that He could possibly give.

139

"The Holy Spirit had been so faithful to Him," she stated. "Jesus depended on Him and He had not let Him down. He said, 'It is expedient for you that I go away: for if I go not away, the Comforter will not come unto you; but if I depart, I will send him unto you'" (John 16:7).

When Jesus said, "And ye shall receive power," He was talking to His own, this great body of believers, not just the 120 in the Upper Room, Miss Kuhlman concluded. "For the promise is unto you, and to your children" (Acts 2:39). "It's for you and me!" she exclaimed.

What was the power that Jesus said would come "when the Holy Spirit has come upon you?" (Acts 1:8). It was the same power that was manifested in His life and ministry.

The greatest gift that Jesus could possibly impart to His church was the gift of the Holy Spirit. "It's a part of your inheritance. It's yours!" declared Miss Kuhlman.

"She Can't Carry a Tune!"

Since Pentecostal manifestations took place in her meetings, Kathryn was often asked about speaking in tongues.

The first time she witnessed someone being filled with the Spirit was early in her ministry when she and Helen Gulliford — "God's Girls" — were traveling together. They were holding a series of meetings in Joliet, Illinois, on the second floor of an old store building. (It was also in Joliet that she became an ordained minister of the Evangelical Church Alliance.)

"I had given the altar call and the service had ended," Kathryn recalled. "There were still about three or four who were kneeling in prayer. It was very late."

One of those who came to the altar for salvation was Isabel Drake, a schoolteacher who commuted every day to Chicago.

"I was sitting there talking quietly with Isabel's mother. Practically all of the lights were turned out — we were saving on electricity."

Suddenly, Isabel Drake, on her knees, looked up, raised her hands toward heaven, and began to sing. "It was the most beautiful song, as clear as a bell. And she was singing in a language I had never heard. It was so ethereal, so beautiful, and I felt the hair on my skin begin to rise."

> "IT WAS THE MOST BEAUTIFUL SONG, AS CLEAR AS A BELL. AND SHE WAS SINGING IN A LANGUAGE I HAD NEVER HEARD."

This was totally unfamiliar to Kathryn. "All I knew when I

first started out in the ministry was salvation, nothing more —
and you do not give to anyone more than what you have
experienced."

The young lady's astonished mother gripped Kathryn's
hand and said, "That's not my daughter singing. She can't even
carry a tune!"

Isabel's face shone like an angel. And as she sang, she was
glorified, magnifying Jesus. This continued for several minutes.

"I was so deeply moved and affected," said Kathryn. "I think
I know a little bit of what the music is going to be like in
heaven. Remember, when the Holy Spirit does it — it is
perfection. There is never a wrong note. It's never flat; it's
never sharp."

That night, for the first time, Kathryn heard singing in the
Holy Spirit.

Hungry for More

Many years later, after Miss Kuhlman's ministry was
revolutionized by the Spirit, she was holding a service in
Portland, Oregon. "A Catholic Sister from the Monastery of
the Precious Light was in the meeting. She had never seen
anyone filled with the Holy Spirit," said Kathryn.

Timidly, the woman came up the steps of the platform and

said, "I've just been healed."

"Oh, Sister, that is wonderful. I'm so glad," replied an exuberant Miss Kuhlman.

As the nun began to walk from the platform, she took a couple of steps, then turned back toward Kathryn and whispered, "I'm so hungry for more of the Holy Spirit."

Kathryn did not pray for the woman, but "in that moment the nun was touched by the Spirit and was lying prostrate under the power. Before she ever hit the floor, she began to speak in the most beautiful language. No one had told her the mechanics." Suddenly, the thousands in that audience became quiet. A holy hush enveloped the crowd.

> "IN THAT MOMENT THE NUN WAS TOUCHED BY THE SPIRIT AND WAS LYING PROSTRATE UNDER THE POWER."

"The angel bent low and that Catholic Sister, who had never been taught how to speak, pray, or sing in tongues, surrendered herself to Him," said Kathryn. "The Holy Spirit was filling her, and suddenly her lips spoke a heavenly language."

It was such a beautiful moment that I'm told Miss Kuhlman felt like taking off her shoes. "We were standing on holy ground," she said, as her memory went back to that moment. "We were standing in the presence of the Most High. The perfection of the Holy Spirit was there."

The Evidence

"How is one filled with the Holy Spirit?" Miss Kuhlman was asked.

She pointed to the Scripture: "He is with you, but He shall be in you" (John 14:17) — and she marked the distinction between the Spirit being "*with* you" and being "*in* you."

It is impossible to ignore that the Holy Spirit is with every Christian, and it begins with His convicting power. "He was even with you *before* you were born again because it is the Holy Spirit who convicts the sinner of sin and of judgment," she preached.

How can the Spirit be *in* you? The reason Kathryn always encouraged people to worship and adore Jesus is because at such a time, the Holy Spirit enters. Jesus said, "He shall glorify me" (John 16:14).

"I believe in speaking in an unknown tongue," she declared. "I believe in it with every atom of my being. But no theologian can show and prove to me in the Word of God that you and I were ever commanded to seek tongues."

The path to being filled with the Spirit, then, is to seek more and more of Jesus. The Holy Spirit comes through praise and adoration. "When you get to the place where you love Jesus with all of your heart it isn't a matter of struggling. It's so easy when you love Jesus to surrender to Him."

Of the two evidences of the Spirit, power and tongues, Kathryn steadfastly maintained that the greater of the two is the power that is manifested in your life. Jesus said, "But ye shall receive power, after that the Holy Ghost is come upon you" (Acts 1:8).

> "WHEN YOU GET TO THE PLACE WHERE YOU LOVE JESUS WITH ALL OF YOUR HEART IT ISN'T A MATTER OF STRUGGLING."

In Miss Kuhlman's view, noise and clamor could never be a substitute for power. She talked about an old, used Model-T Ford she once bought in Idaho for $35. "If noise had been power, that would have been the most powerful thing that ever was on the road," she chuckled.

Jealousy and Pride

To Kathryn, the greatest evidence of having been filled with the Holy Spirit is the fruit of the Spirit that follows. "What good is speaking in an unknown tongue if it is not accompanied by the power of the Holy Ghost and the love of Jesus?"

She pointed her listeners to the words of the apostle Paul: "Though I speak with the tongues of men and of angels, but have not love, I have become sounding brass or a clanging cymbal. And though I have the gift of prophecy, and understand all mysteries and all knowledge; and though I have all faith so that I could remove mountains, but have not love, I am nothing. And though I bestow all my goods to feed the poor, and though I give my body to be burned, but have not love, it profits me nothing. (1 Corinthians 13:1-3).

Miss Kuhlman was disturbed by both the jealousy and spiritual pride she found among many people who claimed to be Spirit-filled. Each is in direct conflict with the Word. "Love suffers long, and is kind; love does not envy; love does not parade itself, is not puffed up" (1 Corinthians 13:4).

She despaired of meeting people who would come up to her and say, "Oh Miss Kuhlman. It's so nice meeting you. I want you to know that I've been filled with the Holy Spirit. I've got the baptism and I've got all the gifts of the Spirit."

Perhaps you too have met people who, after claiming to be filled with the Spirit, become consumed with pride. Everyone else seems to be on a lower level because they have not received "the gift." Kathryn remarked, "I feel like taking a pin and just puncturing the balloon. I get away from that person so fast. Because if you have received the baptism of the Holy Spirit, one of the fruits of the Spirit is humility."

The fruit and the gifts of the Spirit are so sacred, she would never boast about them. She would say, "Like beautiful jewels, they are precious. You guard them so well."

Kathryn maintained that the Holy Spirit is not given for our own enjoyment; it is given for service. "You're misusing this wonderful person if you're using Him for your own pleasure — a little spiritual picnic when you get together with some of the saints of God."

> "LIKE BEAUTIFUL JEWELS, THEY ARE PRECIOUS. YOU GUARD THEM SO WELL."

"I Received It!"

Salvation happens at a specific moment when you are born into the body of Christ. When it comes to the Holy Spirit, however, it is something that is constant and continual. Miss

Kuhlman just shook her head at those who try to exist on an experience that happened long ago and say, "I received it!"

No. It's not in the past, rather it's a daily communing with Him under the anointing of the Holy Spirit. "I don't care what you experienced twenty-five years ago," she would say. "What do you have today?"

> "I DON'T CARE WHAT YOU EXPERIENCED TWENTY-FIVE YEARS AGO. WHAT DO YOU HAVE TODAY?"

She contended that some people are as dried up as last year's corn shucks — trying to still go through the same motions, the same demonstrations. She stated, "I, too, received the baptism with the Holy Spirit, but there is never a time when I am in a great miracle service but what I receive a fresh baptism."

Before I ever preached a sermon, I heard Miss Kuhlman talk about the refreshing power of the Holy Spirit. People marveled that she could stay on her feet for four, five, even six hours in a service without once being seated. What was the key? She stated, "Let me preach an hour under the anointing of the Holy Ghost and I walk off of that platform more refreshed in body and mind than when I walked on."

Speaking personally, I now understand it completely. When the presence of the Holy Spirit descends during a service, my body — regardless of how drained and tired I may have felt — becomes totally alive and revitalized. Great and mighty is the Lord our God!

"He Speaks for Me"

Miss Kuhlman admitted that it was her nature to be impulsive. Yet when it came to the things of the Spirit, she was slow to move — afraid of getting out of God's will. From her own failures she knew the danger of being stubborn, self-centered, and disobedient. That's why she could say, "When you get to the place where you have no will of your own, you cannot miss the will of God."

> "WHEN YOU GET TO THE PLACE WHERE YOU HAVE NO WILL OF YOUR OWN, YOU CANNOT MISS THE WILL OF GOD."

At those moments, when we don't know how to pray, we can turn to the Holy Spirit who knows God's perfect will. "He never works separate and apart from the Father," stated Kathryn. "And He never works separate and apart from Jesus. He has perfect knowledge into the will of God. And when I get to the place I have no will of my own, and I throw myself upon the person who dwells within, He comes before the throne and makes intercession for me and speaks for me."

Give Everything!

"An empty vessel. That's all He's searching for — an empty vessel!"

> "GIVE EVERYTHING OVER TO HIM COMPLETELY — YOUR BODY, YOUR MIND, YOUR LIPS, YOUR VOICE, YOUR CONSCIOUSNESS."

Night after night, after my first encounter with the person of the Holy Spirit, the radio voice of Miss Kuhlman drifted into my Toronto bedroom. Speaking directly to my heart, she said, "Give everything over to Him completely — your body, your mind, your lips, your voice, your consciousness. Yield completely to Him. Remember, all He uses is an empty vessel."

I knew that one encounter with the Holy Spirit was not enough. Each new morning I surrendered myself totally to Him. I prayed, "Spirit of the living God, fall fresh on me." He became my Friend, my Counselor, my Guide.

Yet there was more I needed to learn.

Chapter Eight

The
Secret Power

In the early 1970s I heard a message by Kathryn Kuhlman that left an indelible impression on my life. It was titled, *The Secret Power of the Holy Spirit.*

At the time, I had just come into the Charismatic movement, and frankly, I did not know much about the Spirit-led life. One thing I did know was that I was a hungry young man who wanted everything God had for me.

On the platform that morning, Miss Kuhlman, wearing her usual flowing white dress, preached passionately. I was savoring every word, hungry for more.

After the service I rushed to purchase a cassette and painstakingly wrote down every sentence on a small notepad. I practically memorized the message. It was not an "in one ear and out the other" sermon. This was a message that saturated my thoughts.

Many years later God spoke to me and instructed, "Preach that message."

I questioned, "Lord, it is not my message."

I'll never forget His response. The Lord replied, "You are right. It is not your message; it is My message!"

> I QUESTIONED, "LORD, IT'S NOT MY MESSAGE."

So I preached it because after the years had passed, the sermon was no longer something I had just heard, it was a message I had experienced! *The Secret Power of the Holy Spirit* had become real.

The Great Promise

Kathryn began her message talking about the crowd gathered around the apostles as they came out of the upper room. Peter said, "Repent and be baptized every one of you in the name of Jesus Christ for the remission of sins; and ye shall receive the gift of the Holy Ghost. For the promise is unto you, and to your children, and to all that are afar off, even as many as the Lord our God shall call" (Acts 2:38-39).

The steps to Pentecost could not have been clearer. Peter said, "Repent," then "Be baptized." And "You will receive the gift of the Holy Spirit."

What were the last words Christ uttered before He ascended to heaven? "But ye shall receive power, after that the Holy Ghost is come upon you: and ye shall be witnesses unto me both in Jerusalem, and in all Judea, and in Samaria, and unto the uttermost part of the earth" (Acts 1:8).

What a promise! "You shall receive power." However, it was a conditional promise. The power would not arrive until "the Holy Spirit comes on you." The result of that experience would make you "my witnesses."

When you receive the Holy Spirit, you will not rush out to tell the world about *you*. Instead, you will tell them what Christ is like. You'll have a revelation of Jesus Christ.

What you are communicating is not what a miserable sinner you were and what a great Christian you have become. No. The Holy Spirit is given that you will declare what a mighty God, merciful Savior, and great High Priest you serve.

What is the first step? *Repentance.* It puts you on the road that leads to the fire of Pentecost. Christ said, "I promise you power." That is the destination. But *repentance* is where you must start.

It's Supernatural

The born again experience does not mean that you come to the altar, shed a few tears, say, "I'm sorry, Lord!" and go out the door to live in your sin. That is not repentance. Salvation is a supernatural experience that you cannot accomplish by yourself. It is a gift of the Father, the Son and the Holy Ghost.

> *REPENTANCE*
> MEANS
> CONFESSING AND
> FORSAKING. IT
> MEANS BELIEVING
> AND BEHAVING.

Repentance means confessing and forsaking. It means believing and behaving! You must settle the question of sin — otherwise you will never know the power of the Holy Ghost experience.

So often I see Christians who have literally died on the vine. They have accepted Christ, yet that is the end of their journey. They never receive the promise of the Father. It is the anointing of the Holy Ghost that keeps your salvation alive.

Miss Kuhlman's message that day included much more.

Again and again, however, she returned to that one theme: finding the Holy Spirit begins with repentance.

I remember Kathryn saying, "God has never explained to man the secret of physical birth — then why should we hesitate to accept the birth of the spiritual man? Both come from God." The Word declares, "That which is born of the flesh is flesh; and that which is born of the Sprit is spirit. Marvel not that I said unto thee, Ye must be born again" (John 3:6-7).

A Pair of Bowling Shoes

Miss Kuhlman told a wonderful story which I want to share with you.

As a result of her radio ministry, a twelve-year-old boy named Danny mailed a letter to Kathryn that touched her deeply. He wrote:

> *Dear Miss Kuhlman:*
>
> *Today is my dad's birthday. He said he would like a pair of bowling shoes. That's such an easy gift to give him. But instead of giving my dad what he asked for, I am praying that my heavenly Father will give my dad a birthday present — my dad's salvation. Because you see, Miss Kuhlman, I would rather have my dad give*

his heart to Jesus than anything else in the whole world. I am sending you a picture of my dad at work. One of these days, Miss Kuhlman, I hope soon, I can introduce him to you. He's great.
Danny.

Kathryn looked at the photograph of Danny's father — a handsome man dressed in carpenter's coveralls. "I could tell by looking at him, he would be willing to work his fingers to the bone to earn some money to supply the needs for his young son. He thinks he's being a wonderful dad by paying for the food on the table, buying shoes for the lad's feet, clothes for his body, providing a good home for him, a good bed to sleep in — everything that money can buy."

Instead she saw a father who was missing the mark, "only looking through eyes that have a dollar and cent value."

To Kathryn, the twelve-year-old son had far more wisdom. "A pair of bowling shoes. That would be such an easy gift to give."

Danny wanted his father to have the greatest gift of all — a transformed heart.

It's a Choice

"I know it is wonderful to see sick bodies healed instantly

by God's power," declared Miss Kuhlman, "but there is something far greater. Jesus says, 'You must be born again.' It is not optional."

She also told her listeners that Christ will never force salvation on any person. You come to the Cross because of a personal decision. Scripture says, "Him that cometh to me I will in no wise cast out" (John 6:37).

Kathryn never forgot the day she had to make that choice. On a Sunday in the little Methodist church in Concordia, "no one asked me, no one urged or put pressure on me. Few people who were gathered in church that day knew what it meant to be born again."

In that moment, at the age of fourteen, the Holy Spirit spoke to her heart. "I saw myself a sinner. I saw Jesus as a Savior for my sins and I made the choice — the greatest and wisest choice I have ever made in my entire life. I exercised my will and I chose Jesus as my Savior."

> THE DECISION SHE MADE WAS NOT FOR A DAY, OR FOR A YEAR. IT WAS FOREVER.

The decision she made was not for a day, or for a year. It was forever.

The Bible declares that God does not desire that any

159

person perish or be lost. It is our choice. As Kathryn stated, "There is not a person in hell who can point a finger at Almighty God and say, 'You chose to put me here.'"

When Christ died on the Cross and cried, "It is finished!" a pardon was offered for all humanity. "All you have to do is accept that pardon," Kathryn reasoned. "The option is yours."

Souls! Souls!

Speaking to a convention of the Full Gospel Business Men's Fellowship International, she declared, "I can only tell you that with my conversion there came this terrific burden for souls. When you think of Kathryn Kuhlman, think only of someone who loves your soul, not somebody who is trying to build something. It's only for the Kingdom of God, that's all. Souls! Souls!"

> "I CAN ONLY TELL YOU THAT WITH MY CONVERSION THERE CAME THIS TERRIFIC BURDEN FOR SOULS."

Kathryn's emphasis on salvation had always been at the heart of her ministry. I read a copy of *Joy Bells*, the monthly newsletter she published at the

Denver Revival Tabernacle. In the Easter edition, April 21, 1935, she wrote, "Christ arose from the dead to impart to every believer in Him the full assurance that he is justified in Christ Jesus. Christ Himself promised that He would die to make atonement — and He did. But if God had not raised Him from the dead, we never would have known for a certainty that the atonement had been accepted — therefore He was raised for our justification."

Being born again results in a miraculous transformation, from self to the Savior. Miss Kuhlman said the songwriter had it right when he wrote these three verses:

Some of self, and some of Thee.
Less of self and more of Thee.
None of self, but all of Thee.

One Essential Word

Kathryn Kuhlman's message, *The Secret Power of the Holy Spirit,* has never left me. It is wrapped up in that one essential word — *repentance!* Nothing happens until that condition is met. As David said, "Create in me a clean heart, O God; and renew a right spirit within me" (Psalm 51:10).

To *repent* means, "to turn around." Your heart will no

longer seek the things of the world. Instead, you set your affections on something much higher. Repentance begins by asking Jesus Christ to forgive your sin and continues with a daily crucifixion of the flesh. It is more than saying, "I'm sorry." Rather, it is a daily battle of saying, "No," to self and saying, "Yes," to God.

Have you known the Spirit and somehow lost Him? Get back to repentance. Return to living a crucified life. He will fill you once again with His power — and again and again. You may even reach the point that you will say, "Stop! I just can't take any more."

The Lord is looking for a broken heart. The psalmist wrote, "A broken and a contrite heart — These, O God, You will not despise" (Psalm 51:17). He also declared, "The Lord is nigh unto them that are of a broken heart" (Psalm 34:18).

Jesus spoke of two men who went to the temple to pray. One man boasted, saying, "God, I thank You that I am not like other men — extortioners, unjust, adulterers, or even as this tax collector. I fast twice a week; I give tithes of all that I possess" (Luke 18:11-12). The other man "beat his breast and said, 'God, be merciful to me a sinner'"(v. 13). Then Jesus declared, "I tell you, this man went down to his house justified rather than the other" (v. 14).

A broken heart is the prerequisite, not a crying, defeated

heart that looks to man for strength, rather a repentant soul, ready to receive what God has promised.

When the power of the Holy Spirit came on the apostles, they became giants for God and invaded their world for Jesus. Stephen shook Judea and Samaria. Philip charged boldly into Egypt. They were willing, surrendered, yielded vessels that were changed into strong forces for the kingdom.

> GOD IS WAITING TO RELEASE THAT SAME SECRET POWER OF THE HOLY SPIRIT TO YOU.

God is waiting to release that same secret power of the Holy Spirit to you. It begins with one word.

"Repent!"

After Death — What?

When God began to perform mighty miracles in Kathryn Kuhlman's meetings, it would have been easy for her to change her message. Yet she never did.

In virtually every service she called sinners to repentance. Why? Because she knew that physical healing is temporal, salvation is eternal. In her book *A Glimpse into Glory*, Kathryn answers the question, "After Death — What?"

As long as I'm still in this body of flesh I am susceptible to sickness, disease, sorrow, and heartbreak. It's a body of corruption. It is a mortal body. But one of these days it shall no longer be a vile body. It shall be changed from corruption to incorruption. It shall be changed from mortal to immortal. It shall be raised, not as a vile body, but as a body fashioned like unto His body, the body of our wonderful Jesus.

We thrill to the glorious fact that our sins are covered with the Blood. But my redemption will never be perfected until that day when that which is now corruption, that which is now mortal, shall be raised in incorruption and immortality. One day I shall stand in His glorious presence, with a glorious new body. When the trump of the Lord shall sound and the dead in Christ shall rise first, and those which are still alive shall be caught up to meet Him in the air, so shall I ever be with Him.

Those who have gone before are not lost, not separated from us permanently. One of these days I'm going to see Papa again. One of these days I'm going to see Mama again. One of these days

I'm going to be with my loved ones.

I won't exchange that glorious hope for a title deed to all the world. My place in heaven is prepared. My hope is secure. I'm ready to go. I'll see you on the other side.

For Kathryn Kuhlman, "one of these days" was much closer than she realized.

Chapter Nine

"She Wants To Go Home"

The pressures on Kathryn Kuhlman were enormous. She was adored by countless thousands yet scorned by those who did not understand her calling.

In cities where she ministered, the letters to the editors were often harsh and scathing. "She's in it for the money." "It's a religious scam." "God's not in the healing business." "It's mass hysteria." And anti-Pentecostals took their best shots.

"I invited Kathryn to use our 6,000-seat tent and hold meetings in Akron," Rex Humbard told me. "Suddenly a battle broke out that was on the front page of our paper every day."

He was referring to Dallas Billington, the high-profile fundamentalist pastor of Akron Baptist Temple, who publicly offered $5,000 to anyone who could prove he or she could heal a person through prayer. Of course, the challenge was aimed directly at Miss Kuhlman, who had just opened her meeting. One of the headlines in the Akron *Beacon Journal* read "Healer or Charlatan?"

"The next Sunday more than 18,000 attempted to get into the tent, backing up traffic for miles," Rex recalled.

Kathryn was well prepared. On the platform that day were people from Pittsburgh and Franklin, Pennsylvania, who not only had been healed, they had medical reports to document it.

The conflict was a standoff because Kathryn had always proclaimed that she did not have the power to heal anyone — only God could perform miracles. Billington finally withdrew his offer.

Years later, in Minneapolis, a man volunteered to be an usher at her miracle service. He was actually Dr. William A. Nolen, who was writing a book on paranormal healing. This physician followed up those who claimed to have been healed in that meeting and concluded that each "miracle" could be explained by natural causes.

Several medical doctors rushed to Miss Kuhlman's defense — including Dr. Richard Casdorph, a southern California internist. He and Nolen debated the issue of miracles on the *Mike Douglas Show* in 1975. Dr. Casdorph brought with him Lisa Larios, healed of bone cancer during a Shrine Auditorium meeting, and he had the X rays to prove it. Still, Dr. Nolen would not believe.

Defending Kathryn over the years were a long list of respected medical doctors including Dr. Richard O'Wellen of John Hopkins Medical School and Dr. Robert Hoyt of Stanford University Medical School. Plus, the files at Carlton House were bulging with hundreds of medically-documented cases of miracles.

> "TRUTH DOES NOT NEED A DEFENSE," KATHRYN WOULD SAY, SMILING AT HER CRITICS.

"Truth does not need a defense," Kathryn would say, smiling at her critics.

She also weathered the barrage of attacks from those who believed women preachers are unscriptural.

"I never considered myself a woman preacher," Miss Kuhlman countered. "I am a woman, I was born as a woman and I try to keep my place as a woman. And I try to be a lady. I never try to usurp the authority of a man. Those who know me best don't think of me as being a woman preacher. I am just a person who loves lost souls."

Keys to the City

The controversies seemed minor when balanced with her accolades and achievements.

- In Vietnam, the government presented her with a medal of honor in January, 1970, for building a clinic, a military chapel, and donating 1,200 wheelchairs for disabled soldiers.
- Pope Paul granted her a private audience at the Vatican, lauding her "admirable work." He presented Miss Kuhlman a gold medallion embellished with a hand-engraved dove, the symbol of the Holy Spirit.
- She received an honorary doctorate from Oral Roberts University in 1972.
- The keys to the city of Los Angeles were given to her by Mayor Sam Yorty.

Kathryn had a deep passion for missions. The Kuhlman Foundation built more than twenty church buildings in India, Central America, Asia, and Africa, and donated the facilities to local congregations. Gene Martin directed her overseas projects and more than $750,000 in designated

> KATHRYN HAD A DEEP PASSION FOR MISSIONS.

funds were processed through the Foreign Missions Department of the Assemblies of God denomination. Significant contributions were also made to the Christian and Missionary Alliance world outreach.

When she moved her Friday services to First Presbyterian in Pittsburgh, Dr. Robert Lamont told her, "No, we are not going to charge you for the use of our facilities." The congregation was amazed and appreciative at the sizable donations given to every new church project.

She affected many lives through her support of organizations including the Western Pennsylvania School for Blind Children and the Cincinnati Conservatory of Music. She funded scholarships at Evangel College in Missouri, Oral Roberts University and Wheaton College to provide financial aid to deserving students.

171

Another favorite project was Teen Challenge, David Wilkerson's ministry to rescue young people from violence and drugs.

What the X Rays Showed

Every year Miss Kuhlman's schedule grew tighter. Each week there were at least a dozen major events — television, radio, miracle services, and media interviews, plus a never-ending list of urgent decisions her home office felt only Kathryn could make.

> HER STAFF BECAME GREATLY CONCERNED WHEN SUDDENLY, SHE WOULD STOP DICTATING LETTERS AND LIE ON THE FLOOR.

In 1974 her staff became greatly concerned when suddenly, she would stop dictating letters and lie on the floor. On a flight from Los Angeles to Pittsburgh she was in such pain they rushed her from the airport to her physician. The X rays showed that her heart was greatly enlarged and digitalis was prescribed.

Kathryn should not have been surprised at her problems. Twenty years earlier she had traveled to Washington, D.C. for a physical examination where the doctor diagnosed her heart condition. He warned, "Miss Kuhlman, you are going to have to slow down."

By the summer of 1975 Kathryn was confiding to her closest friends of frequent chest pains. More and more she was in contact with fellow evangelist Oral Roberts.

The Turmoil

Oral first met Miss Kuhlman personally at a 1971 convention where both were featured speakers. As she spoke, he slipped into the back of the auditorium and was genuinely moved. "I knew she was a woman of God," he stated.

The following year she conducted a miracle service at the Civic Center in Tulsa. That's where she met Tink and Sue Wilkerson — he volunteered office space for Kathryn's advance team.

Tink was a successful automobile dealer and a member of the Board of Regents at ORU. His wife, Sue, became a close friend of Miss Kuhlman and they would talk often by phone. The Wilkersons began regularly attending her services across the nation and Tink let it be known to Kathryn that if she ever needed an administrator, he would be ready to help.

At that time the role was filled by Paul Bartholomew, the

173

brother-in-law of Dino Kartsonakis — the flamboyant pianist Kathryn featured in every service and on the *I Believe in Miracles* telecast.

Three years later, in February 1975, a series of traumatic events devastated Miss Kuhlman. First, Dino, the musician who for years had been one of her close confidants — and someone she treated almost like a son — presented her with financial demands she found unacceptable. It was a great disappointment.

Dino immediately was fired and replaced the same day with Paul Ferrin, who began commuting from San Jose, California, where he was on staff at Bethel Temple.

Next, on February 20, she received word that her beloved choir director, Arthur Metcalfe, had suddenly died. Oh, the loss she felt at his passing — not knowing that one year later, to the very day, she, too, would make the same journey.

Once again, she turned to Paul Ferrin as the replacement for Dr. Metcalfe.

In May, she faced an additional dilemma. Paul Bartholomew was a salaried administrator, plus he received large compensation in agency commissions for every television show he placed on stations. Not only was he demanding an extension of his contract, but Kathryn felt his attitude was threatening. She

174

turned to her friend Tink Wilkerson for help.

Bartholomew was soon out of the organization and Tink and Sue Wilkerson were with Miss Kuhlman constantly. The staff in Pittsburgh appreciated the care and attention the Wilkersons were giving to Kathryn, yet they felt a wedge had been driven that separated them from their friend.

THE TURMOIL TOOK ITS TOLL.

The turmoil took its toll.

Looking Back

Knowing what was surely ahead, Miss Kuhlman took time to reflect.

Marjorie Ferrin, who knew Kathryn from her early days in Denver, shared with me a letter she received July 16, 1975. "We have seen God's hand of blessing upon this ministry honoring simple faith — we have seen it grow from a tiny beginning (and no one knows this better than you). The work is not easy, the hours are long, the burdens heavy to carry ofttimes; but when we all stop to look about us and evaluate the accomplishments and results, we feel so well repaid for withholding nothing from Him. It's worth the cost!"

Two months later Kathryn returned to Concordia —

weeping quietly in the cemetery where her mama and papa were buried.

In her book, *Glimpse into Glory,* she wrote, "One day I will have preached my last sermon, I will have prayed my last prayer, and I will stand in His glorious presence. Oh, I have thought of this many, many times, I have often wondered what would be my first words to Him, the One whom I have loved so long and yet have never seen. What will I say when I stand in His glorious presence? Somehow I know the first words I shall say when I look in His wonderful face. 'Dear Jesus, I tried.' I didn't do a perfect job, because I was human and made mistakes. There were failures. I am sorry. But I tried. But — He knows that already."

> "ONE DAY I WILL HAVE PREACHED MY LAST SERMON, I WILL HAVE PRAYED MY LAST PRAYER."

In early November she was billed as the featured speaker at the World Conference on the Holy Spirit in Israel. She came within a breath of canceling because of her failing health. Those near her backstage at the sports arena in Tel Aviv remember hearing her pray, "Dear God, please let me live! I beg

You. I want to live."

Rushed to St. John's

A few days later, Sunday, November 16, 1975, Miss Kuhlman returned to California to conduct her monthly meeting at the Shrine Auditorium. No one knew it, but it would be the last public service of her life. People who were present later told me, "It was as powerful and anointed as any service she ever conducted. It seemed God totally restored her for those few short hours."

Choir director Paul Ferrin recalled, "We knew how sick she was, yet there was a moment when we began to sing *Allelujah*, her entire countenance changed. She became absolutely vibrant."

Following the meeting, Kathryn was rushed back to the Century Plaza hotel, totally exhausted. She became so ill she was forced to cancel her Tuesday morning meeting with Dick Ross, her television producer. Her doctor prescribed medication. Oral Roberts called to pray for her.

To Miss Kuhlman it was unthinkable to cancel her television tapings at CBS the next day. People had flown in to give their healing testimonies and she hated the thought of disappointing them.

Kathryn somehow finished the Wednesday productions, then collapsed in her dressing room. The following day she was in agony, yet struggled through more programs.

By Saturday her stomach was swollen with fluid. The pressure on her heart felt unbearable. A physician was called and Kathryn was rushed to the cardiac care unit at St. John's Hospital. Her blood pressure had dropped below the danger zone and a team of doctors worked for five hours before her condition stabilized. She remained hospitalized.

On December 21 Miss Kuhlman was flown by private jet to Pittsburgh with two nurses in attendance. Despite her critical condition, she was determined to spend the holidays at her Fox Chapel home she loved so well, surrounded by her friends and the works of art that had been given to her over the years.

The day after Christmas, Maggie Hartner received an urgent call from Tink Wilkerson, informing her that the plane would be taking Kathryn to Tulsa. Heart surgery was scheduled at Hillcrest Medical Center, Saturday, December 27. They successfully replaced a defective mitral valve — a valve that controls the flow of blood to the heart.

However, on Friday following the operation, serious complications developed. Over the next two weeks the doctors performed three bronchostomies (to relieve breathlessness)

178

because of problems that had now affected one of her lungs.

Kathryn made a brief recovery, but her strength was almost gone.

Oral and Evelyn Roberts received an emergency call. "You need to come quickly, Miss Kuhlman is slipping away."

> "YOU NEED TO COME QUICKLY, MISS KUHLMAN IS SLIPPING AWAY."

They rushed over to Hillcrest and as they neared the bed to pray, Kathryn lifted her hands as if to push them away, then she pointed up. Evelyn turned to her husband and whispered, "She wants to go home. She wants to go home."

Later that day, February 20, 1976, at the age of sixty-eight, Kathryn Kuhlman was ushered into heaven.

"Take Good Care of Her!"

When the news of Kathryn's death reached me I buried my head in my hands and began to cry. Although I had never met her, Kathryn seemed like a member of my family. She had given me a banquet of spiritual food and her words had inspired me beyond measure. A flood of memories flashed across my mind and all I could do was fall to my knees and pray, "Lord, take good care of Miss Kuhlman. Take good care of her!"

Kathryn's death was a high-profile story in her adopted home city. Reporter Ann Butler wrote in the *Pittsburgh Press,* "What she did was ultimately very beautiful. And there will never be another one like her. She came before the sick and the anguished, those who had suffered, who had lost faith, who had given up — and she lifted them. She made them smile, and she gave them that mysterious, marvelous light of joy in their eyes. She gave them something to believe in. That was her magic."

> "SHE MADE THEM SMILE, AND SHE GAVE THEM THAT MYSTERIOUS, MARVELOUS LIGHT OF JOY IN THEIR EYES."

"It Is Well"

Four days after her passing, 150 invited guests gathered in the chapel at stately Forest Lawn Memorial Park in Glendale, California. Honorary pallbearers included Rex Humbard, Ralph Wilkerson, and Leroy Sanders, pastor of the First Assembly of God Church in North Hollywood, California.

Paul Ferrin was seated at the organ while Jimmie McDonald, through his tears, sang to Kathryn for the last time, *It Is Well with My Soul.*

Oral Roberts was asked to be the main speaker and he accepted — yet he wished the honor had been reserved for someone who had known Miss Kuhlman longer.

In his remarks, Oral said, "Kathryn, as you look into Jesus' face this morning, and you walk down by the riverside, and you see the fruit which is for the healing of the nations, I want you to remember that for a lot of us down here, we're closer to the Holy Spirit than we've ever been." And he added, "We're glad you walked among us, but above all we're glad the Holy Spirit is still walking among us and we're one with you."

Following the funeral service she was buried at Forest Lawn. The bronze marker on her grave reads:

KATHRYN KUHLMAN
I BELIEVE IN MIRACLES
BECAUSE I BELIEVE IN GOD
FEBRUARY 20, 1976

Living Monuments

The tumult that swirled around the last year of Kathryn's

life continued after her death when it was announced that she had signed a new will on December 11, 1975, leaving most of her personal assets to Tink and Sue Wilkerson. That came as a shock to Maggie Hartner and the Pittsburgh staff. The Kathryn Kuhlman Foundation, however, was a separate entity and continues its ministry to this day.

Miss Kuhlman did not leave behind church buildings in Pittsburgh or Los Angeles, nor did she build a school or establish a denomination. She was, however, honored in the town of her birth. When I visited Concordia I saw the historical marker in a peaceful park near City Hall. It reads:

KATHRYN KUHLMAN

BIRTHPLACE, CONCORDIA, MISSOURI

MEMBER OF BAPTIST CHURCH

ORDAINED MINISTER OF THE

EVANGELICAL CHURCH ALLIANCE

KNOWN FOR BELIEF IN THE HOLY SPIRIT

ERECTED 1976

Perhaps her friend Maggie Hartner expressed it best: "There are thousands upon thousands of monuments, but they are not monuments built of brick or stone. They are living monuments, men and women who found Jesus as their personal Savior because Kathryn Kuhlman was true to her Lord in the giving forth of the Gospel."

It was a final tribute to one of God's great servants who would often shrug her shoulders and say, "I just carry a water bucket for the Lord."

Chapter Ten

Unlimited Anointing

People are surprised when I tell them, "I believe God used the anointing that was on Kathryn Kuhlman to carry me until I was ready for mine."

You may ask, "Are you saying you received your anointing from Miss Kuhlman?" Absolutely not! As pastor Ralph Wilkerson remarked after her passing, "Anybody who comes around and says 'I've got Kathryn Kuhlman's mantle,' don't believe it."

I remember the night in 1977 I was at Queensway

Cathedral in my home city of Toronto, ready to speak at what was termed a "film rally." Following her death, the Kathryn Kuhlman Foundation asked me to travel to cities across Canada and the United States for special miracle services. Jimmie McDonald sang, the film of Kathryn's Las Vegas meeting was shown and I would minister.

Since I had watched the film many times, I was walking in a corridor behind the platform, praying — waiting for the presentation to end. During every service, at the conclusion of the film, I would have the audience join me in singing, *Jesus, Jesus, There's Just Something About That Name.*

The moment we began lifting our voices in praise, miracles started happening. People were throwing away their crutches and walking out of wheelchairs! They had been watching a film, we had only sung one chorus and now God was visiting us.

> GOD USED THE TOUCH THAT WAS PRESENT IN HER LIFE TO SUSTAIN ME UNTIL HE PREPARED ME FOR MINE.

I am totally convinced that in those early days of ministry, I was flowing in Kathryn's anointing, not Benny Hinn's. God used the touch that was present in her life to sustain me until He prepared me for mine.

I was a novice, not knowing how to flow in my anointing, yet God gave me the privilege of moving in hers. It was a learning experience which I believe is a scriptural pattern. Joshua followed Moses until he learned how to lead himself. Elisha followed Elijah until his appointed time for ministry.

At McCormick Place in Chicago and in Vancouver, people were being healed during the *film*, even before I walked on the platform. The powerful anointing God had placed on her life was present.

It's Caught!

Again and again people have come to me and asked, "Benny, how can I receive the anointing?" Or they feel God stirring inside of them and say, "I want to receive a double portion!" My advice is to stop waiting in a corner. Get up and move to a place where God's power is flowing. The anointing is not taught, it is *caught* just as an olive can be caught as it falls from the tree.

Don't stay where you are. Look for the anointing and be determined it is going to fall on you. Literally "wrap" yourself in what God has prepared. That's what Elisha did.

The prophet Elijah found him plowing in a field. "Elijah

passed by him and threw his mantle on him" (1 Kings 19:19). From that moment, Elisha was a transformed man. The anointing was so powerful that he slaughtered his oxen and gave the people a free barbecue. He "took a yoke of oxen and slaughtered them and boiled their flesh, using the oxen's equipment, and gave it to the people, and they ate. Then he arose and followed Elijah, and became his servant" (v. 21).

Elisha insisted that the prophet Elijah not leave him. Why? He did not want to be separated from the anointing. When the Lord was about to take Elijah up to heaven and they were on their way from Gilgal, Elijah said to Elisha, "Stay here; please, for the Lord has sent me on to Bethel." Elisha responded, "As the Lord lives, and as your soul lives, I will not leave you!" (2 Kings 2:2).

Next, Elijah told him to stay behind while he went to Jericho. Again, Elisha refused to leave his side (v. 4). And even when Elijah explained that the Lord was sending him to the Jordan river, Elisha repeated, "As the Lord lives, and as your soul lives, I will not leave you" (v. 6).

He wanted to stay close to the mantle — the anointing.

At the river, "Elijah took his mantle, rolled it up, and struck the water; and it was divided this way and that, so that the two of them crossed over on dry ground" (v. 8). When they reached the other side, Elijah said to Elisha, "Tell me, what can

I do for you before I am taken from you?" And Elisha replied, "Please let a double portion of your spirit be upon me" (v. 9).

He desired everything! The prophet explained that what he was asking for was difficult. "Nevertheless, if you see me when I am taken from you, it shall be for you; but if not, it shall not be so" (v. 10).

And, like before, they continued to move on. Remember, God will not give you the anointing unless there is action.

As they were walking along conversing, suddenly a chariot of fire and horses of fire appeared — "and Elijah went up by a whirlwind into heaven" (v.11). But here is the greatest part of the story. As Elijah's mantle fell, Elisha rushed to receive it — he caught the anointing. God allowed him to experience the same power.

> AS ELIJAH'S MANTLE FELL, ELISHA RUSHED TO RECEIVE IT — HE CAUGHT THE ANOINTING.

Scripture records that Elisha returned immediately to the banks of the Jordan. "Then he took the mantle of Elijah that had fallen from him, and struck the water, and said, 'Where is the Lord God of Elijah?' And when he also had struck the water, it was divided this way and that; and Elisha crossed over" (v. 14).

God, in His great sovereignty, arranges times and places when we are near the anointing. Yet if we are blind to it, His touch will pass us by. Don't expect an angel to appear and say, "Hello! I've got something for you."

Elisha kept his eyes open and he caught the mantle.

Great Expectations

Begin to *anticipate* what God is about to do in your life.

Activate your faith and place yourself in a position to receive. That is the advice Naomi gave to Ruth. "Wash thyself therefore, and anoint thee, and put thy raiment upon thee" (Ruth 3:3). If you want to reap the harvest, you must be prepared.

> BEGIN TO ANTICIPATE WHAT GOD IS ABOUT TO DO IN YOUR LIFE.

Rise up and literally anoint your faith. As Isaiah declared, "Arise, you princes. Anoint the shield! (Isaiah 21:5).

Peter and John did exactly that when they were at the Gate Beautiful. Peter looked at a man crippled from birth and said, "Silver or gold I do not have, but what I do have I give to you:

In the name of Jesus Christ of Nazareth, rise up and walk"
(Acts 3:6).

They anointed their faith and they released it. "And he took
him by the right hand and lifted him up, and immediately his
feet and ankle bones received strength. So he, leaping up, stood
and walked and entered the temple with them — walking,
leaping, and praising God" (vv. 7-8).

When I first received the anointing, it was just a drop. The
Lord granted me just a small
touch to see what I would do
with it. As I grew spiritually,
He increased my portion until
today I have a greater measure
than I have ever experienced.

> WHEN I FIRST
> RECEIVED THE
> ANOINTING, IT
> WAS JUST A DROP.

It Must Be Yours

The reason Kathryn Kuhlman placed so much emphasis on
repentance, being cleansed by the blood and living a Spirit-
filled life, is because she knew she did not have the power to
save, heal or deliver *anyone*.

If you turn your back on the Lord and lose His touch, *the
anointing of someone else is not going to save you*. That is the
hard lesson King Saul learned. Samuel told him, "You have

rejected the word of the Lord, and the Lord has rejected you from being king over Israel" (1 Samuel 15:26).

As Samuel turned to leave, Saul "seized the edge of his robe, and it tore" (v. 27). Samuel told him, "The Lord has torn the kingdom of Israel from you today, and has given it to a neighbor of yours, who is better than you" (v. 28). He reached for the anointing, but it was to no avail. Samuel's anointing could not rescue him.

An Infant

In the days when I understood little of the moving of the Holy Spirit, God used the ministry of a woman evangelist to guide my steps. She showed me a pattern to follow — not her pattern but the Lord's.

Today, in our own crusades, there are ministers and lay people who travel hundreds of miles, even from nations all over the world, to be in the atmosphere of the anointing.

I received a letter from a minister in Michigan. "Dear Pastor Hinn," he wrote, "The gifts of the Spirit are new to me, yet every time I return to my pulpit from being in one of your meetings I feel the spiritual tide rising both in me and in my congregation." That is where I was many years ago — a spiritual infant.

Don't be afraid to bring yourself under the shadow of people who are anointed. Let their ministry touch your life. It may come in the form of a tract, a tape, a book, or by physically sitting under their ministry.

Why is this so vital? Because God's Spirit is contagious. Every day, in my own life, in addition to studying God's Word, I continually listen to ministry tapes and read books by great men and women of God. Why? I need fresh oil to be poured on me — from the Lord Himself and from His servants. I continue to read the writings of Wesley, Moody, Finney and the great preachers of history. It keeps the fire of revival burning within me.

> I NEED FRESH OIL TO BE POURED ON ME — FROM THE LORD HIMSELF AND FROM HIS SERVANTS.

Even after Christ had ascended to heaven, His influence did not diminish. The Scribes and the Pharisees could only come to one conclusion. "When they saw the boldness of Peter and John, and perceived that they were uneducated and untrained men, they marveled. And they realized that they had been with Jesus" (Acts 4:13).

Cherish the time you spend in His presence, in His Word and with His people.

I believe the Lord wants you to have more than a double portion, for there is no limit to the anointing of the Holy Sprit. I believe He wants to pour out an *unlimited* anointing upon His children.

Don't delay the journey.

Chapter Eleven

Allelujah! Allelujah!

In the late 1960s, when the Vietnam War protesters and the flower-children of Haight-Ashbury were in full bloom, the "Jesus People" were winning thousands of young people to the Lord.

Jimmie McDonald remembers the day when about 200 who were part of this movement came to the CBS studios for a taping of one of Kathryn's television programs. "Some thought they were just long-haired hippies," he recalled.

While they were waiting for the *I Believe in Miracles*

production to begin, they began singing a chorus, *Allelujah, Allelujah.*

No one on Miss Kuhlman's staff had ever heard it before. Says McDonald, "Kathryn felt such a power in that song that she immediately called for an extra program to be taped. They gathered around the piano and sang it — again and again."

From that day forward, in almost every service Miss Kuhlman conducted, the song was included. It became a tradition in her services.

Today, in our own crusades we sing *Allelujah, Allelujah.* It is more than a simple refrain, it is a powerful entry into worship.

People who attended Miss Kuhlman's services are often surprised when they visit one of our meetings and find we are singing much of the same music.

He's the Savior of My Soul.
Spirit of the Living God, Fall Fresh on Me.
How Great Thou Art.
Jesus, Jesus, There's Just Something About That Name.
He Touched Me.

These songs are not only timeless, they carry with them rich, deep meaning, bringing people into the very presence of God.

McDonald, who has participated in many of our crusades, recalled the first time he ever sang in one of Miss Kuhlman's meetings. "I was astounded at how people entered into the service," he observed. "People sang *How Great Thou Art*, more powerfully than I had ever heard. It was because so many who were worshiping had personally been delivered and touched by the Holy Spirit."

When God's mighty power began to move it touched Jimmie McDonald deeply. He recalled, "Many nights, when I sang *He Touched Me*, I could never make it through the song because of what I saw happening in the lives of people."

The Lord uses everything — music, messages and manifestations — to bring people closer to Himself. Yet there is something that takes place *before* a service ever begins that is a vital key to God's blessing. It is *prayer.*

> THE LORD USES EVERYTHING — MUSIC, MESSAGES AND MANIFESTATIONS — TO BRING PEOPLE CLOSER TO HIMSELF.

Always Prepared

I remember asking Maggie Hartner, "Tell me about

Kathryn's prayer life. Did she pray in the mornings? Late at night? Was it before the services?"

She replied, "People find this hard to believe, but Kathryn prayed *all* the time."

> "I'VE LEARNED TO COMMUNE WITH THE LORD ANYTIME, ANYPLACE."

Miss Kuhlman once told David Wilkerson, "I take my secret closet with me — if I'm in a car, that's my secret closet, or wherever I am. There's nothing in the Bible about being in a geographical place or location to pray. I've learned to commune with the Lord anytime, anyplace."

When a reporter asked Kathryn, "How much time do you spend preparing for a miracle service?" she answered, "You don't understand, I *stay* prepared. You don't prepare for a service. I'm prepared twenty-four hours of the day." Then she added, "I say to my ushers at the services, 'Listen now, this is no time to have a prayer meeting — you come prayed up before you get here!'"

Ralph and Allene Wilkerson told me, "We can't count the number of meals we ate together, but one thing we will never forget. Kathryn did not care for idle conversation; her entire focus was on the ministry and the services. Food wasn't even important!"

"Please Help Me!"

When some people pray all they think about are their personal failures and needs. "Lord, forgive me." "Please help me!" It's all "me, me, me."

Of course we must confess our sins and seek God's guidance, yet we need to understand that prayer is communing with the Lord — listening to and talking about the things that are on His heart. We need to love Him, thank Him, worship Him, and enter into His presence. Our needs will be met in *His* time, not ours.

By receiving the Lord's warmth, tenderness, and wisdom, we move into obedience to His voice — and that is the key to the anointing of the Holy Spirit. He will entrust you with small things to determine your faithfulness. Then, if you are loyal with a little, He will entrust you with more, enabling you to fulfill the calling He has placed on your life.

The Lord does not respond because of your excellent vocabulary or words of knowledge. No! He pours out His anointing because He sees a heart that truly longs to know Him. The psalmist wrote, " The Lord is near to all who call on

Him, To all who call on Him in truth." (Psalm 145:18).

Kathryn once remarked, "You would be amazed how many people write to me and ask, 'Will you please send me the prayer that you prayed?'"

To her, communing with God was infinitely more than saying prayers. It was something that welled from deep inside — nothing written out or memorized. "A printed prayer can sometimes help you become God conscious, or create an attitude of prayer," she remarked, "but that is not really praying. You must realize that prayer involves a relationship with God."

Constant Praise

Miss Kuhlman not only prayed constantly, she *praised* constantly, obeying Paul's charge to "Pray without ceasing, in everything give thanks; for this is the will of God in Christ Jesus for you" (1 Thessalonians 5:17-18).

During a message she delivered entitled *The Whole Armor of God*, she inquired, "Have you come before the throne of God without asking for anything, just spending ten or fifteen minutes adoring the Master, telling Him how much you love Him, praising Him and thanking Him for His blessings and goodness to you?"

Kathryn knew the secret to real prayer: coming to the Lord in praise, worship, adoration and with a grateful heart. She believed it was possible "to constantly live in the spirit of thanksgiving, our hearts grateful for God's goodness, mentally thanking Him for His blessings and protection." And in the midst of life's duties, even when we are in a conversation with someone, "we can be conscious of a spirit of gratitude within our heart and mind."

A Burning Fire

It is wonderful to reflect upon the times in your life when God came and blessed you in a special way. However, is that still happening? Is the fire still burning within you? Is God continuing to give you revelation knowledge? The Word says, "But ye have an unction from the Holy One, and ye know all things" (1 John 2:20).

The anointing from above is your source of knowledge. That is how it is possible for you to operate in revelation rather than in education.

> THERE IS NO SUBSTITUTE FOR GOD'S FRESH OIL.

There is no substitute for God's fresh oil. It will lift the burden you are carrying and will break the bondage that hinders your life. Isaiah wrote, "And it shall come to pass in that day, that his burden shall be taken away from off thy shoulder, and his yoke from off thy neck, and the yoke shall be destroyed because of the anointing" (Isaiah 10:27).

God wants you to become a burning fire aglow with the Spirit. He desires that you come alive again by the touch of His mighty hand. "Let thy head lack no ointment" (Ecclesiastes 9:8). Get ready for God's transforming touch. Receive a fresh infilling daily.

Are you ready to receive what God has in store? Or are you complacent and satisfied with something that may have happened yesterday?

David received his first anointing and seemed headed for a lifetime of becoming Saul's slave and playing the harp to keep away the demons. Then he received his second anointing and became king of Judah. Finally, he received his *third* anointing and was crowned king of Israel. That is when dominion and authority were given to the former shepherd boy. It was then that he took Mount Zion.

You will never realize the authority God wants you to have unless you progress beyond the first anointing. It is when He *continues* to anoint you that you begin to know His mighty power. Remember that Jesus "breathed" on the disciples, then came Pentecost. Later in Acts 4, the power fell, the building shook and they began to speak the Word with boldness! Multitudes were added to the Church.

"We Want Nothing"

Those looking for Miss Kuhlman's secret to opening the flood gates of heaven didn't have to search far. In a miracle service she lifted her head to the Master and prayed, "We vow to give You, Lord Jesus, the praise for all that happens in this place of worship. We vow with our very lives to give You the glory. We want nothing, Lord Jesus, to inhibit our praise of You, not our circumstances, not finances, not troubles, successes, or things. We praise You, Lord."

> *Enter into his gates with thanksgiving,*
> *and into his courts with praise:*
> *be thankful unto him, and bless his name.*
> *— Psalm 100:4*

Allelujah! Allelujah!

Chapter Twelve

"Yes, Lord. I Will!"

Do you believe God speaks through dreams? I do.

Several years ago the Lord visited me in a dream so real I can see it to this day.

It began as I slowly walked into a beautiful building that had three rooms. As I entered the door of the first room, there was Kathryn Kuhlman — just as I remembered her, in a flowing white dress.

Miss Kuhlman looked straight into my eyes and said, "Follow me."

Together we walked into the second room, and standing before us was Jesus, the mighty Son of God.

As the dream continued, Kathryn vanished — she simply disappeared. Now I was alone with Jesus, Who spoke, saying, "Follow Me."

I followed the Lord into a third room. Before me was a man who was crippled and paralyzed. A tube was inserted in his throat. As the Lord walked toward the man, he was instantly and totally healed.

> BEFORE ME WAS A MAN WHO WAS CRIPPLED AND PARALYZED.

Then Jesus looked at me and spoke two words with great power and authority, "Do it!" But the Lord did not disappear. He remained with me in the room.

I awoke from that dream, humbled and crying, "Yes, Lord. I will!"

A Little Book

Being obedient to God does not guarantee a smooth road or the absence of trials. Often it's quite the opposite. Followers of Christ have been ridiculed, persecuted and thrown into prison.

Kathryn once recalled the day she picked up a little red book she had read many times as a child. She opened the volume and found she had scribbled some thoughts in the back of the book. She said, "I am wondering now whether I fully understood what I was writing at that time, for I was not more than sixteen or seventeen years of age."

Here are the words she wrote:

Whether life grinds a man
down, or polishes him depends
on what he is made of.

A diamond cannot be polished without
friction, nor man perfected without trials.

Great pilots are made in rough waters and deep seas.

Closing the book, Kathryn turned back the pages of her life. "Years have come and years have gone since that moment," she said, "and I can bear witness to the fact that every word I wrote that day is true. I believe it is because of those deep waters, the storms, the winds, the gales, that I am the person I am today."

Decades earlier, when she faced that "dead end" street in Los Angeles and thought her life was over, the Lord knew exactly where she was. He sent the Holy Spirit to give her a new vision that forever changed her future.

God also knows where *you* are.

I remember the night in 1975 when Kathryn came to London, Ontario, and I volunteered to sing in the choir. I wanted to be close to everything that was happening. I was twenty-three and had been preaching for less than a year, still trying to understand God's calling on my life.

After the meeting, as I was walking across the platform to locate the friends I had arrived with, Miss Kuhlman's choir director, Paul Ferrin, grabbed my arm and stopped me. He said, "Sir, I don't know who you are, but God has His hand on you and I want to pray for you." And he did.

Paul probably forgot that incident, yet it was a significant moment for me. It was a confirmation that the Lord was guiding my steps.

It's Coming!

Don't believe it when you hear that the Church is dead or dying. God is calling out His "servants and handmaidens" as never before and miracles are taking place in every corner of the world. It is only the start!

Here is the prophecy that has already been partially fulfilled and is now about to be completed: "And it shall come to pass afterward, that I will pour out of my spirit upon all flesh; and your sons and your daughters shall prophesy, your old men shall dream dreams, your young men shall see visions" (Joel 2:28).

God is about to release an anointing of His power that has never before been experienced. The coming outpouring can only be described as being without measure. To this point, what we have received has a dimension that allows us to measure and compare. What is on the horizon is as immeasurable as the universe. It will be given to those who have been faithful with what they have already received. Jesus said, "He who is faithful in what is least is faithful also in much" (Luke 16:10).

Signs Following You

What the Lord foretold in the last chapter of Mark is about to explode on an unprecedented scale. "These signs shall follow them that believe" (Mark 16:17). You will no longer be following signs — signs will be following you. The demonstration of God's power will be flowing like a rushing,

> YOU WILL NO LONGER BE FOLLOWING SIGNS — SIGNS WILL BE FOLLOWING YOU.

209

mighty river.

"In My name they will cast out demons" (v. 17). The coming anointing will give you total power over the enemy.

> THE COMING ANOINTING WILL BUILD A FORTRESS OF SECURITY AROUND GOD'S PEOPLE.

"They will speak with new tongues" (v. 17). The mighty army of Spirit-filled believers has grown to untold millions — and the power is increasing.

"They will take up serpents; and if they drink anything deadly, it will by no means hurt them" (v. 18). The coming outpouring will build a fortress of security around God's people.

"They will lay hands on the sick, and they will recover" (v. 18). When this great anointing falls, you will pray for people and instantly see them healed.

How is the Lord going to pour out His Spirit on all flesh? Through you! Through me! The world is going to say, "These Christians have turned the world upside down!"

A Mighty Visitation

The Lord wants you to receive, function, flow, and live in the anointing. It is not for a spiritual "high" but for service. Be ready! The Master is about to return. He is going to look into your eyes and ask, "What have you done with what I have given you? Have you received the Holy Spirit whom I have sent?"

The anointing will give you a new authority. If "one chase a thousand, and two put ten thousand to flight, "(Deuteronomy 32:30) just think of what happens when it multiplies.

The prophet Daniel said those who "know their God shall be strong, and do exploits" (Daniel 11:32). Through God's servants the world will be reclaimed and changed from a place of desolation into a land of beauty. "The wilderness . . . shall will rejoice and blossom as the rose. Then the eyes of the blind shall be opened, and the ears of the deaf shall be unstopped. Then the lame shall leap like a deer, and the tongue of the dumb sing. For waters shall burst forth in the wilderness, and streams in the desert" (Isaiah 35:1,5-6).

What a mighty visitation! And the Lord wants you to be part of it! When the fullness of God's Spirit falls, you will feel like the Psalmist when he declared, "Let God arise, let his enemies be scattered" (Psalm 68:1).

One day Satan will have mounted his last attack. Jesus said,

211

"All power is given unto me in heaven and in earth" (Matthew 28:18). It will never be given back to the enemy.

What God is preparing is not just for today, but for eternity. You will rejoice "forevermore."

> WE MAY BE INTERESTED IN FILLING BUILDINGS, YET GOD IS CONCERNED WITH FILLING HEAVEN.

The next event on God's calendar is the return of Christ. The outpouring of His Spirit on your life is to prepare you for that moment — and to give you power to share the Good News with the world. I have never been more convinced about the Second Coming than today.

The clock is running out.

We may be interested in filling buildings, yet God is concerned with filling heaven. And He can only accomplish the task by filling you.

Will It Be You?

Each time I think back on the life of Miss Kuhlman, I realize how God uses ordinary people to accomplish His purpose. Again yesterday, I was inspired as I listened to one of her messages.

David Wilkerson wrote in the foreword of her book, *Nothing is Impossible with God*, "History will say of Kathryn Kuhlman: her living and her dying brought glory to God."

What will be the story of your life? How will you respond when the Lord gives you a vision for your future and says, "Do it!"

It matters not where you were born, the circumstances of your life or the mistakes you have made. The eyes of God are searching the world for a willing vessel He can mightily use — someone, *anyone*, who will totally yield themselves to His Holy Spirit.

Will that someone be you?

Index of Names

References

Jamie Buckingham, *Daughter of Destiny* (Plainfield, NH: Logos International, 1976).

Larry Keefauver, editor, *Kathryn Kuhlman's Healing Words* (Lake Mary, FL: Creation House, 1997).

Helen Kooiman Hosier, *Kathryn Kuhlman* (Old Tappan, NJ: Flenming H. Revell, 1971).

Roberts Liardon, *God's Generals* (Tulsa, OK: Albury Publishing, 1996).

Roberts Liardon, *Kathryn Kuhlman* (Tulsa, OK: Albury Publishing, 1990).

Kathryn Kuhlman, *A Glimpse Into Glory* (New Brunswick, NJ: Bridge-Logos Publishers, 1983).

Kathryn Kuhlman, *An Hour With Kathryn Kuhlman* (Pittsburgh, PA: The Kathryn Kuhlman Foundation). Audio cassette.

Kathryn Kuhlman, *Baptism of the Holy Spirit* (Pittsburgh, PA: The Kathryn Kuhlman Foundation). Audio cassette.

Kathryn Kuhlman, *Gifts of the Holy Spirit* (Pittsburgh, PA: The Kathryn Kuhlman Foundation, 1981).

Kathryn Kuhlman, *God Can Do It Again* (South Plainfield, NJ: Bridge Publishing, Inc., 1969).

Kathryn Kuhlman, *Great Pilots Are Made In Rough Seas* (Pittsburgh, PA: The Kathryn Kuhlman Foundation, 1987).

Kathryn Kuhlman, *The Greatest Power in the World* (North Brunswick, NJ: Bridge-Logos Publishers, 1997).

Kathryn Kuhlman, *I Believe in Miracles* (Englewood Cliffs, NJ: Prentice-Hall, 1962).

Kathryn Kuhlman, *In Tribute to Kathryn Kuhlman* (Pittsburgh, PA: The Kathryn Kuhlman Foundation, 1980). Audio cassette.

Kathryn Kuhlman, *Lord, Teach us to Pray* (Pittsburgh, PA: The Kathryn Kuhlman Foundation, 1988).

Kathryn Kuhlman, *Nothing is Impossible With God* (South Plainfield, NJ: Bridge Publishing, Inc., 1974).

Kathryn Kuhlman, *Victory in Jesus, and The Lord's Healing Touch* (Pittsburgh, PA: The Kathryn Kuhlman Foundation, 1986).

Jimmie McDonald, *The Kathryn Kuhlman I Knew* (Shippensburg, PA: Destiny Image, 1996). Audio cassette.

Wayne E. Warner, *Kathryn Kuhlman: The Woman Behind the Miracles* (Ann Arbor, MI: Servant Publications, 1993).

The official Kathryn Kuhlman archives are permanently housed at the Billy Graham Center on the Wheaton College campus in Illinois.

The Kathryn Kuhlman Foundation

I would like to express my thanks to the
Kathryn Kuhlman Foundation for their continuing
efforts to touch lives through the ministry she began.
To receive a list of Kathryn Kuhlman's books, tapes
and videos which are available, contact:

The Kathryn Kuhlman Foundation
P.O. Box 3
Pittsburgh, PA 15230
(412) 882-2033

For more information on other resources
from Benny Hinn, please write or call.

By mail:
Benny Hinn Ministries
P.O. Box 90
Orlando, FL 32802-0090

By phone, 24 hours a day, seven days a week:
To order resources: 1-800-433-1900
For more information: 407-292-4200

In Australia:
Benny Hinn Media Ministries, Australia
P.O. Box 2422
Mansfield, Queensland 4122
Phone: 7-33433977

In Canada:
Benny Hinn Media Ministries, Canada
P.O. Box 638, Station U
Toronto, Ontario M8Z 5Y9
Phone: 905-501-0115

In the United Kingdom:
Benny Hinn Media Ministries, Ltd.
P.O. Box 20
Bedford MK41 OZZ
England
Phone: 44-1234-262644